BEAUTIFULLY RESILIENT

BEAUTIFULLY RESILIENT

THRIVING THROUGH MENTAL ILLNESS WITH GOD, MY TOOLBOX OF COPING SKILLS, COMMUNITY, FAITH, AND FRIENDS

AMY DIANE STEWART

XULON PRESS

Xulon Press
555 Winderley Pl, Suite 225
Maitland, FL 32751
407.339.4217
www.xulonpress.com

© 2024 by Amy Diane Stewart

All rights reserved solely by the author. The author guarantees all contents are original and do not infringe upon the legal rights of any other person or work. No part of this book may be reproduced in any form without the permission of the author.

Due to the changing nature of the Internet, if there are any web addresses, links, or URLs included in this manuscript, these may have been altered and may no longer be accessible. The views and opinions shared in this book belong solely to the author and do not necessarily reflect those of the publisher. The publisher therefore disclaims responsibility for the views or opinions expressed within the work.

Unless otherwise indicated, Scripture quotations taken from the Holy Bible, New Living Translation (NLT). Copyright ©1996, 2004, 2007 by Tyndale House Foundation. Used by permission of Tyndale House Publishers, Inc.

Disclaimer: I am not a medical professional. I have lived with mental health experience. Try these skills at your own risk. I am not liable or at fault for any suicide or homicide. With that said, I wish you the best.

Paperback ISBN-13: 979-8-86850-434-1
Ebook ISBN-13: 979-8-86850-435-8

Table of Contents

Dedication vii
Letter to the Hurting ix
Introduction: Imagination is Key xi

Part 1: Into the Heart of Chaos 1
    Chapter 1:   Life is Not a Slice of Apple Pie 2
    Chapter 2:   Only Jesus Christ Can Take the Leper and Let
                     Her Stand 6
    Chapter 3:   The Start of Something Scary 8
    Chapter 4:   A Time of Testing 12
    Chapter 5:   Shame off Me 17

Part 2: Mental Illness, the Tools I Use, and the Community
Behind Me 21
    Chapter 6:   Transformation Through Psychoeducation 22
    Chapter 7:   Casting My Cares On God 25
    Chapter 8:   Warning Signs, Triggers, and Learning Experiences . . . 28
    Chapter 9:   My Emergency Toolbox for Stress 31
    Chapter 10: The Importance of Community as a Social
                     Support System 38
    Chapter 11: The Struggles of Work 43

Part 3: Where My Faith Comes Alive 47
    Chapter 12: Compassion: A Call to Action 48

    Chapter 13: I Want to Be like Jesus, David, Paul, Mary, and Ruth... 51
    Chapter 14: Helping You Become a Child of God...a Personal Decision to Follow Christ 53
    Chapter 15: Healing Rain 56

Resources... 59
    Characteristics of Who We Are In Christ 60
    Encouraging Verses from the Bible............................ 64
    Struggling and Needing Resources?........................... 70

Appendixes.. 77
    Appendix A: If You Knew the Real Me...…................... 78
    Appendix B: My Testimony 79
    Appendix C: Letter to Self Written While Hospitalized in 2012 .. 87
    Appendix D: Prophecy by Jane Hamon, an Author and Prophetess, on Feb 27, 2008..................... 89
    Appendix E: Prayers to God while in the 12 Step Program 92

Acknowledgements 92
Speaking to Social Workers for a Second.... 103
References 106

Dedication

To God (Yahweh, my heavenly father – my Abba, the Son – Jesus Christ, and the Holy Spirit) for getting me through these tough years and showing me who I truly am in Him, especially as His daughter! I would not be here without you!

To my Mom, thanks for always having wisdom regarding my abuse. You have tried to understand me and my illnesses and made me feel seen. You were there with me through the good and bad and still loved me. I love you too!

To my Mom and Chad for learning how to love me for who I am as a child of God.

To my friends at Eagle's View Church, thank you for all the prayers, late-night talks, encouragement, and support! I have loved, laughed, and cried more in the past few years than ever before. Tapestry, Regeneration, and Hope Ministries have pulled me through this with God's help. To our pastor, who taught me that it is okay not to be okay. I gain strength from your testimony and sermons.

To my social workers and psychiatrist, I would not have made it here without y'all. Thanks for never giving up on me, even in the deadly valleys. The mountaintop experiences are now amazing.

Letter to the Hurting

Sometimes, we stumble into doubting or asking why. However, on other days, we have it all together. All we want is to be free from our captivity, which is talked about in Isaiah. I know you have done all you could, so please reach out your hand to the one who writes the day. We need God to love us. So, put your trust in Him as you look to the future. Jesus Christ will come back. Hold on, my friend, because better days are coming, so do not give up. We should realize that Jesus Christ is the way, the truth, and the life. He is calling out to you. He tells us we are not alone because He is always there and will be for all eternity. He reminds us that when we are overwhelmed and our worlds start falling apart, He will never leave nor forsake us. He stays beside us and shows us that strength comes when we are down on our knees. We should remember the promises that He gave us. We need to realize that the cross was enough. Trust me, there is a place waiting that we will call home. It will be worth it because everything works for our good, even if God did not cause bad things to happen. Even though we are unworthy, it is all right because we are made holy by Jesus Christ's blood. God's unconditional love takes sinners like us and puts Jesus Christ's righteousness on us. After all, you have the power you need to change your legacy, having a faith that causes us to change because there is joy inside with the love of God. What if we learn to love our brothers and sisters for nothing in return? We could reach out to those needing help and treat them better than ourselves. What if we somehow changed the world? After all, you could be a hero and change the world. You no longer have to be afraid because we are the light, hope, and love worth fighting for.

I hope that one day, you will accept your illness and understand that it does not define you. I hope you make peace with why things happened the way they did because mental and physical illness are not anyone's fault; after all, you survived this and more. I hope you love yourself enough to forgive yourself if you should experience a relapse in your mental health recovery process by having patience with yourself. Learn to smile and breathe again. Maybe one day, you will look at yourself with love and admiration and learn to trust yourself again. Perhaps you will discover how to love and be loved again. I hope you stay humble, kind, and compassionate while forgiving yourself and others, and always be authentic. This is my prayer for you.

With much love,
Amy

Introduction: Imagination is Key

*P**salm 34:18: "The Lord is close to the brokenhearted; he rescues those whose spirits are crushed."* Imagine with me for a second. There I am on the loneliest wet day in San Antonio in February 2005, just staring out my window, rocking back and forth. I remember days when I would cry for part of the night and sleep all the next day. I had trouble making friends and could not work or volunteer. The hardest part was not asking for help because I thought I did not deserve it and that I was worthless and unlovable. I was the most depressed I had ever been. Well, this is a reality for many people who have schizoaffective disorder.

I have fought through dark nights that were lonely and scary and lived to tell about it. I have fought voices in my head, flashbacks, and intrusive memories. I have lost friends who died by suicide and fought my own dark demons regarding that. I might have lived with mental health experience, where I have fought tooth and nail to survive, but that has made me a more compassionate, caring, and loving person. I have found that if I stick to a regimen of medicine, have a routine schedule, get sleep, eat healthier, go on walks in nature, and do lots of self-care and self-love, I am normal (if there is such a thing). I am a growing and learning adult who happens to have schizoaffective disorder–bipolar type, and complex Post Traumatic Stress Disorder. Can stigma be overcome? I believe it can, one person at a time. Let us start with me.

Imagine God saying, "I am here, and I love you." It took me years to get to this place. I looked at God as angry and harsh. I did not truly see God as a healer and life-giver until I overcame my fear and shame. I had to stop relying on my feelings and stand on the promises of God. I knew I might not be cured, but I could learn to manage my illness. I had to remember to trust God. It was no longer why but who. I had to open my mind to a living and loving God. I acknowledged my illness and realized we lived in a fallen world of free will. God was not to blame. I thought God had been against me for a long time, but now I see Jesus Christ entering my storms with me.

Sometimes Christians say to me to "pray more," "stop sinning," "I should forgive everyone," or "I do not need to be healed with medical assistance." They do not know that I already pray continuously, forgive constantly, and am being transformed to be more like Jesus Christ. The only exception is being off my medications, which I cannot do, and they last for a lifetime. I wish I could express to you that this is a brain disorder, like any other illness in your body, like diabetes or cancer. You should have a holistic approach. God shows He cares when He gives me excellent counselors, a psychiatrist who understands me, access to medication, and a community that loves and encourages me. I hope you know God is close by, cares for, and comforts you while encouraging and loving you.

On another note, God calls Christians to compassion and love in action and word. The Church should love people who struggle with mental health concerns, especially brothers and sisters in Christ, regardless of their struggles. I know we would greatly appreciate it.

I want to remind you that God, others, and I love you. I know things are hard right now, and that is okay. You do not have to do this alone. Do what you can right now, and no more than that. That is all God expects of you. You are a child of God. I am listening, and we are here for you. You are never a burden, and I care for you. This book will tell you about the toolbox

Introduction: Imagination is Key

I have used to cope with schizoaffective disorder (bipolar type), Complex PTSD, and borderline personality disorder (BPD). These are suggestions, and I hope they help. With God, all things are possible. I hope this helps you find the necessary tools and resources to succeed. I hope to inspire you to discover what works for you because everyone is different. It is about development and improvement from the trials we encounter.

PART 1
Into the Heart of Chaos

CHAPTER 1
Life is Not a Slice of Apple Pie

Philippians 2:1-4 "Is there any encouragement from belonging to Christ? Any comfort from his love? Any fellowship together in the Spirit? Are your hearts tender and compassionate? Then make me truly happy by agreeing wholeheartedly with each other, loving one another, and working together with one mind and purpose. Do not be selfish; do not try to impress others. Be humble, thinking of others as better than yourselves. Do not look out only for your own interests, but take an interest in others, too."

Sooner or later, it happens – something goes terribly wrong. Perhaps there is a knock at your door, a phone call in the middle of the night, a particular tone in your doctor's voice, or a pink slip on your desk. In a single moment, trouble can unexpectedly come and turn your world upside down – leaving you dazed, confused, and wondering why.

I have had many hospital visits in the middle of the night and made phone calls no young person should make. What about the tone in a doctor's voice? Doctors have told me that I would not make it through the night. Why do I have hyponatremia and low thyroid levels anyway? High blood pressure and high cholesterol followed me through my twenties. How about being told by different psychiatrists that you would not make it past your twenties due to suicidal ideation and self-harm?

Sometimes, I feel broken and afraid, like my strength fails me, and tears finally come out. Despite the journey's length and the road's adversity, the legacy of those who came before me inspires me to continue. As I feel God's presence, I know He is with me. As His grace and mercy pour over me, I will get on my knees and praise the God who gives and takes away. I am God's beloved.

Why does life bring us trouble? Trouble often comes at the invitation of our poor choices. However, the Book of Job teaches us that trouble sometimes comes because we have done something right. What do you believe trials are for? In Romans 5, it talks about how trials build our character. I think trials prove our faith and prepare us for service. How we act in discouraging situations will reflect what we believe. The Apostle Paul proved his faith even in paralyzing times. The real purpose of life is to love, serve, honor, and glorify God. Thank goodness it is not for personal fulfillment or based on how I feel. That makes me cringe. What about people reading John 3:16 but missing verse 17, which builds it up? *John 3:16-17: "For this is how God loved the world: He gave his one and only Son, so that everyone who believes in him will not perish but have eternal life. God sent his Son into the world not to judge the world, but to save the world through him."* Praise God for His love, grace, and mercy. Just remember that God truly loves you but does not cause suffering. The Christian life is messy and complicated work. It involves getting rid of things that might harm our relationship with God. What about Hebrews when it talks about running with endurance? *Hebrews 12:1-2: "Therefore, since we are surrounded by such a huge crowd of witnesses to the life of faith, let us strip off every weight that slows us down, especially the sin that so easily trips us up. And let us run with endurance the race God has set before us. We do this by keeping our eyes on Jesus, the champion who initiates and perfects our faith. Because of the joy awaiting him, he endured the cross, disregarding its shame. Now he is seated in the place of honor beside God's throne."* Focus on who is at the table with you: Jesus Christ himself. Do not get distracted by yourself or the circumstances surrounding you. Do not lose sight of the opportunity: eternity with Jesus Christ himself.

I prayed to God to help me grow. He taught me how to forgive others and myself, to love my enemies—no matter what happened—serve with humility, bring honor and glory to Himself, pray constantly and consistently, work with all my heart, and bless others generously. That is what I have learned. Thank You, God! Praise You, God!

> *Romans 5:1-5 (NLT): "Therefore, since we have been made right in God's sight by faith, we have peace with God because of what Jesus Christ our Lord has done for us. Because of our faith, Christ has brought us into this place of undeserved privilege where we now stand, and we confidently and joyfully look forward to sharing God's glory. We can rejoice, too, when we run into problems and trials, for we know that they help us develop endurance. And endurance develops strength of character, and character strengthens our confident hope of salvation. And this hope will not lead to disappointment. For we know how dearly God loves us because he has given us the Holy Spirit to fill our hearts with his love."*
>
> *James 1:2-4 (NLT): "Dear brothers and sisters, when troubles of any kind come your way, consider it an opportunity for great joy. For you know that when your faith is tested, your endurance has a chance to grow. So let it grow, for when your*

endurance is fully developed, you will be perfect and complete, needing nothing."

1 Peter 1:3-9 (NLT) "All praise to God, the Father of our Lord Jesus Christ. It is by his great mercy that we have been born again, because God raised Jesus Christ from the dead. Now we live with great expectation, and we have a priceless inheritance—an inheritance that is kept in heaven for you, pure and undefiled, beyond the reach of change and decay. And through your faith, God is protecting you by his power until you receive this salvation, which is ready to be revealed on the last day for all to see. So be truly glad. There is wonderful joy ahead, even though you must endure many trials for a little while. These trials will show that your faith is genuine. It is being tested as fire tests and purifies gold—though your faith is far more precious than mere gold. So when your faith remains strong through many trials, it will bring you much praise and glory and honor on the day when Jesus Christ is revealed to the whole world. You love him even though you have never seen him. Though you do not see him now, you trust him; and you rejoice with a glorious, inexpressible joy. The reward for trusting him will be the salvation of your souls."

CHAPTER 2

Only Jesus Christ Can Take the Leper and Let Her Stand

Zephaniah 3:17 "For the Lord your God is living among you. He is a mighty savior. He will take delight in you with gladness. With his love, he will calm all your fears. He will rejoice over you with joyful songs."

Behavior is how someone acts. It is what a person does to make something happen, change, or keep things the same. For example, in the Psychology Dictionary[1], these "actions, activities, and processes are started in response" to my internal thoughts and feelings and my external ones, like the environment and others.

When in my right mind, I can change what I do, how I do it, what I say, and how I say it, but not without struggle. I do this mainly by taking thoughts captive, especially negative ones, and changing them to positive ones, then growing as a human being. This has taken a few decades to learn. It also took a support system who had me by the hand and guided me.

When my mental illness is in play, it is much more complicated to change my behavior since it is a brain disorder. There is the irrational and

---

[1] "Behavior." APA Dictionary of Psychology. American Psychological Association, Accessed January 1, 2024. https://dictionary.apa.org/behavior.

unreal. You assume that I can control my mind, thoughts, and actions. What about hallucinations, delusions, paranoia, and impulsivity? What about overwhelming fears? What happens when you lose control of your mind?

Growing up, I buried things deep inside, hid secrets, and stayed silent. I had to bear my pain alone and learn to rely on no one. I learned to turn my emotions off when it got too painful to feel. I learned to put on a smile and wear a mask. I could not cry because it was a disappointment. I became so invisible that my feelings did not matter. I died a little each day until I nearly shattered. As time passed, I was careful about who I let in my life and had difficulty trusting myself and others, even God. Sometimes, I was a people pleaser with low self-worth. My nightmares and flashbacks intimidated and drained me. I struggled with codependency in relationships with an innate feeling of shame. I was not able to tolerate conflict and overly agreed with everyone. What about my fear of abandonment, rejection, and betrayal? I craved external validation while putting my needs aside for others, and I always feared what might happen next and sometimes tolerated abusive behavior while earning love. I felt excruciating pain when people hurt me, and I often blamed myself. I felt anger and hopelessness when I told myself they could change. I frequently felt battered and used because I spent years wasting my time on them. I meant nothing to them, so why didn't I realize this sooner? They did not deserve me in the first place.

Why can't I see that freedom is sometimes simply another perspective away? My friends adore me, but my parents think I should change. Who could I be if my lens was altered for a moment? Would I still be the same? Can I honestly tell you that no one else could understand all of the hurt inside? Look at the world and all the suffering in it. Is my life so bad? There is nothing wrong with needing help sometimes.

CHAPTER 3

The Start of Something Scary

Isaiah 41:10 "Don't be afraid, for I am with you. Don't be discouraged, for I am your God. I will strengthen you and help you. I will hold you up with my victorious right hand."

When I was nineteen years old, I was diagnosed with schizoaffective disorder, bipolar type, quiet borderline personality disorder, and complex post-traumatic stress disorder. One of these diagnoses would be disheartening, but they all nearly destroyed me. I thought I was going to die. I felt like everything was my fault. I felt like I was worthless and unlovable because that is what the voices told me. I would sit all day watching TV and talking to my voices. I thought people were out to get me, and the government was planning my demise. I was having flashbacks of abuse and dying on the inside. I was talking in my sleep and having terrible nightmares. I thought the whole world was caving in on me. I struggled with suicidal thoughts, actions, and feelings. I finally talked with my mom and decided to go to the hospital. I remember self-harming while in the hospital because I wanted to punish myself. For a while, I went between loving people and hating them. I had the intense lows of depression—sadness, emptiness, and feelings of worthlessness—and the highs of mania—shopping sprees, irritability, and racing thoughts. I had disorganized thinking and made up words a lot. I even had dissociation, feeling like I was disconnected from myself and environment, as if not in my body. I had a fear of abandonment and rejection and intense anxiety. I had chronic feelings of boredom and emptiness. I had uncontrollable anger toward others, and that scared me. Worst of all were the self-hate thoughts.

I remember thinking cutting would take all the pain away. It was only a temporary fix. I felt numb and empty. Sometimes I wanted to release intense feelings, try to break through emotional numbness, avoid distressing memories, or punish myself. I was so confused. After signing an agreement with my counselor, I attempted to stop but found it a cycle. I tried everything from ice on my skin to popping rubber bands on my wrists. I felt so much shame from it. The only person who could heal me from it was Jesus Christ. I had to come up with better coping skills with my hands due to my impulsive behaviors. One thing that helps me is CARESS[2], a coping strategy that helps me regain my sense of emotional and physical control. The CA stands for Communicate Alternatively, where I can express and understand my feelings by painting or writing. The RE stands for Release Endorphins, where I release endorphins by walking fast, watching babies laughing or funny animal videos, or hugging my pet. The SS stands for Self Soothe, where I enjoy rocking in a rocking chair while wrapped up in a blanket, taking a candle-lit bubble bath, listening to soothing music, or a relaxing exercise like deep breathing.

Regarding self-harm, recovery is possible but tricky. For someone with a mental illness, impulsivity can be a challenge. What makes me feel the need to do it? Often, it is punishment or numbness and usually after dealing with abuse, abandonment, rejection, neglect, or betrayal. The scars remind me of

---

[2] Ferentz, Lisa. "USING CARESS TO WORK WITH SELF-DESTRUCTIVE BEHAVIORS." The Ferentz Institute. Accessed January 1, 2024. https://www.theferentzinstitute.com/2021/03/15/using-caress-work-self-destructive-behaviors/.

where I have been. Why didn't someone warn me to save me from myself? My heart was broken, and I was ashamed, which I used to be so tired of. My heart was so heavy. After three decades of verbal and emotional abuse and my mental illnesses, I struggled to want to live. I had lost my will to fight. I thought I was defined by my illness, choices, past mistakes, and the problems I created. I built my walls so high that God had to take them down brick by brick.

Regarding my suicidal ideation, it is more of my schizoaffective disorder than in my control. Some days, the ideation is too much to handle. I did attempt to end my life twice but decided that suicide was not the condition under which I wanted to meet God. Some of my symptoms included withdrawing, having mood swings, feeling trapped, sleeping too much, being hopeless, and being severely anxious. I sought help immediately and encourage you to call a suicide hotline like 988 or go to the nearest emergency room when suicidal. At one point, I did have my mom remove unsafe items from our home. I am thankful for the friends who offered me an opportunity to talk about my thoughts and feelings and encouraged me. It did not push me into doing something destructive. God intervened and provided comfort in my time of crisis, not condemnation. He is the mighty comforter for every kind of pain. Take your pain to Him; He wants to listen and help.

It took me years to break the cycle of depression and suicidal ideation since, with my mind, there is trouble with memory and concentration. I took every thought captive and replaced it with scripture from the Bible, like *Romans 12:2: "Don't copy the behavior and customs of this world, but let God transform you into a new person by changing the way you think. Then you will learn to know God's will for you, which is good and pleasing and perfect.",* which talks about being transformed by the renewing of your mind. I practiced every day until I had it down. I did this by using a spiral of who I am in Christ, which was a horizontal purple spiral with animal stickers, positive affirmations, and the Bible Verses to back the affirmations up, and I would open it daily and focus on who God says I am. My thinking was transformed as I accepted that God loves and cares for me. It does not mean I will never have negative thoughts again. Believe me, I still do, but now I can better manage my thoughts and feelings. Jesus Christ is the way, the truth, and the life, and He saved me. I am accepted, forgiven of all my sins, secure, free from condemnation, significant, and chosen in Christ. Thank you, Jesus Christ!

Sometimes, after practicing taking thoughts captive, there are some quiet moments of peace in my head where I sit, self-reflect, and process, but it is not a pity party. I feel God's presence, but He is silent, and it is beautiful. We sit there and feel each other's presence in peace.

CHAPTER 4
A Time of Testing

> *James 1:2-4 "Dear brothers and sisters, when troubles of any kind come your way, consider it an opportunity for great joy. For you know that when your faith is tested, your endurance has a chance to grow. So let it grow, for when your endurance is fully developed, you will be perfect and complete, needing nothing."*

I have known abuse, neglect, abandonment, rejection, and mental illness for as long as I can remember. I will admit to struggling with a sense of stability sometimes. I once had a social worker ask me if I liked being sick as if it were a choice. For so many years, I wondered why I could not choose to tell the difference between what was real and not real. However, when people I know calmly explain to me that they cannot see, hear, feel, taste, or touch the sensation I am describing, it is helpful when done without an accusing manner. Now, I can generally tell whether or not a voice is from God or is a hallucination. God is loving and kind, and there is no condemnation in Christ Jesus. Everything God says is backed up by Scripture. Usually, my other voices are command hallucinations and always telling me to do bad things, which is me and not God. Sometimes, with severe visual hallucinations, I would try to reach out and try to touch them, which did not always work and often left me depressed. With both my internal and external auditory hallucinations, I have tried talking with them and get to know them, especially since so many of the voices are just versions of myself. I have befriended my inner child and work with her regularly. I have worked with my command hallucinations, which usually are voices that tell me to do bad things, with courage, often fighting with my Dad's voice, which is now better. My friends in the past have pulled me out of delusions, but I fought so hard because it seemed so real. Over time, the anti-psychotic medications I was taking and counseling with cognitive behavior therapy would quiet all of these, especially when I learned about my triggers like stress and how to cope with it. I even joined mental health support groups. Currently, I am learning how to sit with my emotions and be uncomfortable since I no longer dissociate, and I try to stay in the present. I often get bored and feel empty with very little pleasure. There are no more voices or paranoia, and I do not think I am someone that I am not (delusions), but sometimes I still have mood swings and anxiety, and I even deal with intolerable personal hygiene some days. I am starting to learn more about myself and have more interests and choices, which I never really had before. I need to find contentment while being stable. I try to fill my days with volunteering, having fun with friends, and attending college online. Please hear me: There are so many factors that lead to a person's story, like genetics, brain chemistry, environment, and holistic health, but I did not choose my mental illnesses, nor would I wish them on my enemies if I had any. Stigma is horrible, and my mental illnesses do not define me.

Currently, I have some good days and lots of bad days. I often wonder if anyone will be able to understand where I am coming from. I deal with stigma a lot in my world. What people do not understand is that there are days when I wish all this turmoil with my mental illness would end. I wonder what it would be like to be in Heaven and not have a care. However,

I know suicide is not how I want to meet God. I do not always like having insight into my illness because, on hard days, it can be quite confusing. Understanding that you are having a hallucination or being told you are having a delusion as it happens can be debilitating. There are many days that life is lonely and depressing when all you want is for the pain to stop. My mood swings sometimes rapidly and other times slowly over a period of days. It is hard to explain the impulsivity of my disorder. Sometimes, my impulsivity is so strong that I hurt myself. I have to find a healthier coping skill than self-harm. Something that uses my hands since they sometimes shake uncontrollably. I love painting by numbers and coloring, but there are some days that I cannot do them. I used to have some putty, which helped. I also cannot always go on a walk, especially at night. These times when you cannot control the illness wear on you heavily. Some days, the torment is too much to bear. However, I must remind myself of the good days, which give me hope. These days, my friends pick me up and encourage me to keep going. These days, I celebrate small victories because I have accomplished my goals. Days where I volunteer in the community because I have love and compassion for the people I meet. Then, I remind myself that I do not have it so bad, and the day starts over.

Sometimes, people ask me about my bad days. Some days are filled with brain fog, which feels like a buzzing sensation in my head where my thoughts stop, and there is no thinking. On other days, I am emotional, whether that be depressed or manic. Most days, I am really quiet, like a mouse. I keep everything inside and overthink way too much. I do not get angry much anymore. Since building my toolbox of coping skills to manage Borderline Personality Disorder and bipolar disorder, I have calmed down over the years. So, let's be honest. You will not have emotion-free days, you will probably always hear voices, and you will likely always deal with paranoia. People often use black-and-white thinking when it comes to emotions, thinking that all emotions are bad or all emotions are good. You think of God without emotions, but I laugh at this. This is the same God who courageously parted the Red Sea, laughed with the disciples, dropped sweat of blood in the Garden of Gethsemane, and cried with Mary and Martha over Lazarus's death. We act like God never gets sad or fearful of losing people to Satan when our future with God is our choice. Every single life has dignity and worth. No one is too far gone or too lost. So why do we act like it? Be there for them. Just listen with no words. Hold and comfort them as they fear the future. I know I dread the future even though I am saved. It is like not being able to control the fear in my life. This does not mean I do not trust God; it just means I do not control my future with my mental illness. I know the answer: God is always there and loves me unconditionally. When you have a mental illness, it creates self-doubt, and often, I question whether He loves me. Thankfully, the doubting usually brings me back to God because I know I would not be here without Him. God is so comforting. The days I crawl in His arms and rest are amazing. He cries with me and even laughs with me too. I truly treasure the moments He spends with me.

Regarding feelings and emotions, I can be either numb or overwhelmed. Furthermore, my bipolar side is intense with depression and mania. Most of my mood disorder is mainly depression, and has moved away from mania over the years. Over the years, I have taken my mania and learned to manage life while making a purpose for its good side. I turn anger and irritability into positive coping skills like volunteering or cleaning my room. There are still some days I deal with self-hate, where the weight of the world seems too much to bear. Sometimes, the memories and flashbacks are too much, and the fear of failing again seems overwhelming. Sometimes, it is hard to breathe, so I remind myself that anything is possible with God by my side. I remind myself of the freedom found in Jesus Christ. I was lost, but now I am found. God is for me. I am chosen. I am so loved that He made a place for me in Heaven. Who am I? I am a child of God.

> Step 1 to talking to someone self-injuring:
> **Give someone the space to talk.**

CHAPTER 5

Shame off Me

> *Hebrews 4:15-16 "This High Priest of ours understands our weaknesses, for he faced all of the same testings we do, yet he did not sin. So, let us come boldly to the throne of our gracious God. We will receive his mercy and find grace to help us when we need it most."*

To heal from the wounds of the past, I had to face the fact that my past was painful. There was an impact on my relationships, both past and present. I have experienced mental, verbal, emotional, sexual, physical, and spiritual abuse. In my situation, my loved one used gifts and told me to keep them secret, and it started with a harmless touch. There were a lot of threats and emotional manipulation. I felt different as a child and stuffed down my emotions. I internalized the abuse and blamed myself, which I felt I deserved. Control was not mine. June Hunt states, "Emotional abuse is any ongoing, negative behavior used to control or hurt another person (Hunt 9)[3]." People in my life have used emotional abuse when they had unrealistic expectations, demeaned family members, tried to intimidate me, and humiliated and shamed me publicly. It was when I was called stupid, crazy, a beached

---

[3] Hunt, June. Verbal & Emotional Abuse: Victory Over Verbal and Emotional Abuse. Fifteenth Edition. California: Rose Publishing, 2016.

whale for being overweight, and told I would never make it. The belittling, bullying, and degrading inflicted immense pain and heartache. I felt worthless and unloved for three decades. I no longer knew who I was. My confidence was crushed. My sense of self-worth wore away. They damaged my sense of dignity and God-given worth. I went to counseling for decades. I acknowledge their brokenness and need for the love and forgiveness of Jesus Christ and me because all have sinned and fallen short of God's glory. Not until 2021, in a local 12-step program for overcoming hurts and habits, did I learn to forgive them. I am still working on forgiving myself. I am learning to have loving and trusting relationships. I realize that I have been living a lie, believing that I am to blame for being mistreated and believing that my happiness will come from human relationships. I have a choice about being around anyone who mistreats me. I do not want to have a false loyalty to anyone who abuses me. Nor do I want to have the false expectation that the abuse will stop if I can change. I will no longer live for the approval of others but will rely on the Lord to meet my inner needs because my value and worth come from Him, and He loves me unconditionally. Only the Lord can meet my needs. After all, I was able to confront the problem with empathy. I told a specific loved one I forgave them for deeply hurting me. I now see them from God's viewpoint. Christ died for them, and they have God-given worth. To combat my shame, I have a network of friends who care about me and support me spiritually and emotionally. I had to be honest to God and others about my anger, bitterness, unforgiveness, and hate, which were sins. I also sought forgiveness from my mom and stepdad for taking the abuse I suffered out on them. I asked God for forgiveness and a compassionate heart that was sensitive toward others who have experienced abuse. In my 12-step group, I wrote the loved one a letter and later burned it. I also use a spiral I came up with about who I am in Christ.

An after-effect of the abuse was shame, which became my identity. Shame is like a pervasive weed that tries to choke the life out of the people it touches. Shame told me that I was worthless, unlovable, a failure, and a mistake. According to Edward Welch, who wrote *Shame Interrupted*, "It is any rejection, neglect, or demeaning words by someone who is supposed to love you" (Welch 14)[4]. For me, it was the gradual sum of words and actions. On top of the abuse, I believe this loved one abuses alcohol. I was called horrible things, felt different from others, and felt responsible. I needed love and acceptance. This is where God comes in.

God is attentive to the excluded, forgotten, burdened, and outsiders. He invited me into His kingdom and was faithful to me because of His love, not my worthiness. I have sinned, and there is forgiveness available to sinners. Trust in Jesus, in His words and promises, because of who He is, what He has said, and what He has done. I belong to God and have a purpose (Jeremiah 29:11). His love and faithfulness will endure forever (Psalm 117:2, Psalm 100:5). As I turned away from the actions of people that once defined me and turned to God, I found acceptance, honor, and worth. I stand forgiven and holy before God because Jesus Christ took the penalty for my sins on Himself and gave me His holiness and righteousness.

Everyone has a past. It is what you do with it that matters. All the wrong choices and the abuse I suffered left me in pieces. I gave away my heart effortlessly and had my hopes crushed too often. This was when the failures of my life brought me to my knees. Shattered, shamed, and troubled, I still kept fighting. With not many people to help, I looked up and turned to God. It hurt worse than anything I had ever experienced, but God helped lead me out of the darkness. Despite the pain and failures, I still had hope and belief. That is when I found my strength and courage in Jesus Christ. I know I had

---

[4] Welch, Edward T. Shame Interrupted: How God Lifts the Pain of Worthlessness & Rejection. First Edition. North Carolina: New Growth Press, 2012.

to go through all this to become who I was meant to be as a child of God. No matter how small, these steps in this book were some of the hardest I have ever known. No matter what happens or how hard things get, I understand there is nothing God and I cannot handle together. I kept going and growing. I started celebrating what makes me unique. I hope this is true for you, too. I can be a strong and confident woman while being encouraging, caring, and graceful. You can be everything God says you are in Him. Remember His faithfulness.

> Step 2 to talking to someone self-injuring:
> **Invite them to talk about
> what is causing their pain.**

PART 2
Mental Illness, the Tools I Use, and the Community Behind Me

CHAPTER 6

Transformation Through Psychoeducation

Proverbs 3:5-6 "Trust in the Lord with all your heart; do not depend on your own understanding. Seek his will in all you do, and he will show you which path to take."

In my twenties, I had the opportunity to learn about my illnesses from NAMI's Peer-to-Peer Program, and I attended for several weeks. There, I learned what schizoaffective disorder was and the symptoms that went with it. Through this class and my experiences, I learned how to manage and cope with my illness.

I learned that the illness requires ongoing, permanent management and is caused by biological (genetics), environmental, brain function, and developmental factors. I was given anti-psychotics, mood stabilizers, and anti-depressants. I felt like I lived in a brain fog most of the time with unwanted side effects. Over the years, I would go through medication after medication. Sometimes, the medications did not work, or stopped working, and my symptoms reoccurred. I eventually settled on Risperidone as my anti-psychotic, with Trileptal as a mood stabilizer and Wellbutrin and Zoloft as my anti-depressants. I have been on medication since high school and have been in therapy even longer, and I am a strong advocate for both medication and therapy.

I have had both cognitive behavior therapy and dialectical behavior therapy, both types of psychotherapy (talk therapy). Heather Jones[5], a mental health professional, describes, "CBT is one of the most common forms of evidence-based psychotherapy. It helps a person identify and change maladaptive thought processes and behaviors. CBT typically involves: learning to reevaluate negative thought processes, relaxing the body and calming the mind, confronting instead of avoiding fears, developing healthy coping skills, and building self-confidence and self-esteem. DBT is an evidence-based treatment that is derived from CBT. DBT encourages experiencing and accepting the emotions and developing healthy ways to cope with them. The four key components of DBT are: cognitive behavioral theoretical framework, validation, dialectics (when two seemingly opposite things are true at the same time/the integration of seemingly opposing viewpoints), and radical acceptance (accepting that pain, stress, and other negative things may happen, but you have the tools to cope with them)(Jones 2022)." They both work, and I encourage you to seek help if you need it. My Christian counselor reminded me what my Lord and Savior, Jesus Christ, had done for me (dying for my sins so I could have eternal life with Him). We slowly did CBT and went through my life story and started changing negative thought patterns and making them positive. She explained throughout my time there that the abuse was not my fault. She taught me how to manage my mental illness. I learned self-care tips (exercising, 8 hours of sleep, eating healthier), learned how to distract myself in crisis (DBT – Distress Tolerance), learned communication skills (listening, speaking, observing, and empathizing by

---

[5] Jones, Heather. Dialectical Behavior Therapy vs. Cognitive Behavioral Therapy. Very Well Health. October 15, 2022. https://www.verywellhealth.com/dialectical-behavior-therapy-vs-cognitive-behavioral-therapy-uses-benefits-side-effects-and-more-5323767

active listening, friendliness, empathy, and respect), learned to be determined (built self-confidence and self-esteem), practiced deep breathing exercises (breathe in for 4 seconds, then hold 4 seconds, then exhale 4 seconds) and mindfulness (staying in the present time while observing one's thoughts and feelings without judgment), placing a weighted blanket on me to calm down (DBT), and wrote in a thoughts/feelings journal ("clarity and insight into your own patterns of thinking and behavior" – Van Horn 2023[6]). To forgive others, I wrote many letters stating my feelings and then burned them. I learned to take baby steps, set simple goals, and have patience with myself and others. I also learned compassion and love for others and myself. Celebrating small victories with friends, family, and my counselor is crucial to going forward. My most significant breakthrough was accepting that my past and my mental health concerns do not define me. Resilience is my style.

> Step 3 to talking to someone self-injuring:
> **Listen until they are done sharing.**

---

[6] Van Horn, Hannah. Journaling About Feelings: How to Explore and Express Emotions. April 26, 2023. https://dayoneapp.com/blog/journaling-about-feelings/

CHAPTER 7

Casting My Cares On God

1 Peter 5:7 "Give all your worries and cares to God, for he cares about you."

I have lived with mental illness for decades. So, what made a difference for me in beating my symptoms to create a fulfilling life? Acceptance, medication, peer support, counseling, coping skills, self-care, love, and engagement in a Christian community have helped me. My acceptance was over time and was not fast or easy but challenging. Over time, I had to grieve the image of who I wanted to be, what kind of life I expected, and what I wanted to have. I had to come to terms with not being entirely in control of my mind or path in life. It took me a while to grieve because I was so numb and often dissociated. I have accepted that there is no cure and that this illness may be long-term. I want to remind you that you are not alone and can get through this. I once saw a quote by Christine Yu Moutier, Chief Medical Officer of the American Foundation for Suicide Prevention, saying, "Recovery is an ongoing process of healing and discovering and practicing new strategies to thrive (Duckworth 158)[7]." I agree with this. Life is a journey, not the destination, with its mountains and valleys.

---

[7] Duckworth, Ken. *You Are Not Alone: The NAMI Guide to Navigating Mental Health*. First Edition. New York: Zando, 2022.

The Bible talks about casting your cares on God, for He cares for you (1 Peter 5:7). I once heard it explained like a fisherman casting his fishing net. It is a throwing of all burdens and cares upon God because He can handle them and truly cares. God delights in taking them. He is an Almighty Warrior who can crush Satan and, at the same time, gently comfort you. No problem is too big or too small for Him. I love coming to Him when I feel like a burden because He is kind and caring. He never turns you away or hurts you. He even rocks me to sleep while I'm crying. He is a loving and compassionate Father.

Sometimes, I still struggle with feelings of emptiness. Over the years, I have had to encourage myself to praise and worship God through the pain. I did not feel like it, but I could not rely on my feelings. I chose to trust God's Word, which is truth. He loves me and will never leave nor forsake me (Deuteronomy 31:8)! Some of my best worship comes when I realize that God will be with me by my side even in my loneliness and neediness! Joy is not the absence of pain but praising God through it. Worship is a posture of the heart with the reassurance of salvation and the presence of God enveloping you. Please hear me. I am not trying to minimize my situation. All of my most significant breakthroughs are due to the Holy Spirit. He is there to lead and guide me through the pain.

Now and then, fears of abandonment and rejection creep up, too. Sometimes, I have a fear of failing or being out of control. I worry about what would happen if I had another episode when I have gotten so far. To combat this, I remind myself that I am a child of God. I use a flip spiral index card notebook with verses about who I am in Christ. I remind myself that I am adopted, chosen, and loved by the Creator of the Universe. Also, God sent His Son to die on the cross for all our sins, and I am forgiven by Jesus Christ's birth, life, death, resurrection, and ascension. These things give me great comfort.

> Step 4 to talking to someone self-injuring:
> **Always be non-judgmental and offer support.**

CHAPTER 8

Warning Signs, Triggers, and Learning Experiences

2 Corinthians 4:8-9 "We are pressed on every side by troubles, but we are not crushed. We are perplexed, but not driven to despair. We are hunted down, but never abandoned by God. We get knocked down, but we are not destroyed."

Warning signs like hallucinations and delusions can be seen after less severe symptoms begin, like getting words confused or making them up, a lack of pleasure, and concentration symptoms. If you detect any of these signs or symptoms in yourself or a loved one, the best thing you can do is call 988, an emergency assistance line for suicide, or go to the nearest emergency room.

Some common warning signs are diminished job or school performance, difficulty concentrating, paranoia or suspicion of others, reduced self-care like hygiene, isolation or spending more time alone, and intense emotional responses or a lack of emotions (National Institute of Mental Health 2023)[8]. I also experienced dissociation, fatigue, memory loss (which became better

---

[8] National Institute of Mental Health. (2023). Understanding Psychosis (NIH Publication No. 23-MH-8110). U.S. Department of Health and Human Services, National Institutes of Health. Retrieved April 23, 2023, from https://www.nimh.nih.gov/health/topics/schizophrenia/raise/fact-sheet-early-warning-signs-of-psychosis

through therapy and medication), lack of sleep, lack of appetite, extreme sadness and anxiety, shame, anger, racing thoughts, lack of motivation, irritability, negative self-talk, and restlessness.

Triggers can lead to flashbacks, nightmares, and intrusive memories. Sometimes I am triggered by something I or others do or say. Examples of triggers are holidays, birthdays, anniversaries, seeing some loved ones, seeing people drink, stress, anxiety, loneliness, frustration, anger, disappointment, guilt, shame, boredom, low self-esteem, self-pity, peer pressure, free time, isolating myself, feeling overwhelmed, being criticized or judged, and lack of confidence.

What have I learned over the almost two decades of living with my mental health concerns and my treatment?

We often learn that who we are and what we do are two very different things. We might hear voices, too, but that does not mean you should be scared of us. We are not who you see on TV or at the movies. Those are typically overdone. We do have "normal" lives by taking our medicines and going to doctor and therapy appointments. We might share a condition, but we are not the same. I hope you realize that every disorder is different for everyone. If you do not understand our illness, accept us for who we are as a child of God. We are not drama queens, attention seekers, or crazy people. Our minds are wired differently, and we have a mental health condition that is managed. Sometimes, we may react negatively when we feel misunderstood or upset, but it is because we need a better emotional release. Furthermore, sadness is not the same thing as depression because depression is so much more than that. Plus, being exhausted does not make us lazy. We are kind, loving, and caring once you get to know us.

Choosing to stay focused on the future while putting the past in its place, I am choosing to move forward. Learning body awareness and benefits from mindfulness, I have been able to cry and let my emotions out, especially after talking to family members about the abuse and realizing I was not the only one. Social support has also helped, especially talking with a family friend who has been through trauma. Even reenacting and experiencing me telling this loved one to stop has brought a sense of completion. After intellectually realizing where the past needs to go in my life story, I do not fear others as much and feel safe with certain people. At this time, my PTSD has quieted, giving me long enough to heal. As I started reflecting on myself, I learned to have compassion for myself and even started to love myself more. I choose not to let this loved one or my mental health concerns define me. I am even liking myself more, especially since I have gone back to school to help others, volunteering, and writing a book. I have used mindfulness, deep breathing, grounding techniques, and video-guided meditation as coping mechanisms. My community supports me, and I even am appreciative of my meds and taking them daily. I have a meaning and purpose and am not mad at God anymore. I choose not to project the men in my life on God and His character. The past few weeks have been cathartic, and the timing is perfect. Plus, I know the answers. I just have to translate it from my brain to my heart. I am actually at peace with myself.

> Step 5 to talking to someone self-injuring: **Make sure to focus your questions on the emotional triggers preceding the self-harm and the effects following it.**

CHAPTER 9

My Emergency Toolbox for Stress

"Be gentle with yourself. You are a work in progress. So give yourself the grace to grow. Never lose hope because one day you will thank yourself for not giving up." – Anonymous

Sometimes, I have to take life moment by moment. If that means just brushing my teeth or making the bed, those baby steps are essential. Celebrating small victories with friends and family is crucial to going forward, and I want to improve my quality of life.

Sometimes, I make lists to remember things. Setting the alarm for medications and a calendar for appointments also helps bring structure and routine. Set small, simple recovery goals to achieve at your own pace and celebrate the small successes.

Self-care is essential. I exercise regularly, get at least eight hours of sleep, and try to eat healthy. Since stress is my greatest trigger, I like to relax while taking bubble baths, taking naps, doing paint-by-numbers, hanging out with family and friends, watching movies that make me smile or laugh, and reading the Bible. I also like to write in a gratitude journal and praise the Lord while listening to worship music.

At home, I have an emergency toolbox that I use when in distress. In it, I have word search books to keep my brain sharp, adult coloring books with colored pencils to calm my anxiety, a journal of thoughts and feelings, and brochures on mental health from the National Alliance on Mental Illness. I also have some personal growth items like a small Bible, Bible Promise Book, and a book by Max Lucado entitled "God Thinks You Are Wonderful." Some different mementos include "get well soon" cards, a letter I wrote to my future self, my testimony printed out, pictures of family and friends, and a spiral notebook of Bible verses about who I am in Christ. One of my most used objects is my music for every emotion. I listen to Christian rock like Kutless or Sanctus Real when I am angry and Christian pop music like Mercy Me and Matthew West to calm me down. My all-time favorite is worship music to lift my spirit. Art therapy and music help me a lot, especially as coping skills that help me process thoughts and emotions. Sometimes, there is a shift and change in my mood. When depressed during winter, I use a light therapy box light that helps me stay grounded. I also practice healthy boundaries when needed. Establishing and maintaining boundaries are setting healthy boundaries (a psychological demarcation that protects the integrity of an individual or group or that helps the person or group set realistic limits on participation in a relationship or activity[9]) that help protect your mental and emotional health. For example, if you tell someone "no" and they cross the line, you can have consequences like not doing something for them.

Cognitive Behavioral Therapy is "any theory deriving from general behavioral theory that considers cognitive or thought processes as significant mediators of behavioral change[10]." "CBT is an evidence-based psychotherapy that helps a person identify and change negative thought processes

---

[9] "Boundary." APA Dictionary of Psychology. American Psychological Association, Accessed January 1, 2024. https://dictionary.apa.org/boundary.

[10] "Cognitive Behavior Theory." APA Dictionary of Psychology. American Psychological Association, Accessed January 1, 2024. https://dictionary.apa.org/cognitive-behavior-theory.

and behaviors. (Jones 2022)[11]" I still use cognitive behavioral therapy as well. I keep a feelings journal, write letters stating my feelings, uncover automatic thoughts, and using my spiral notebook for who I am in Christ (positive affirmations with Bible verses to back it up). Cognitive behavioral therapy taught me how to take self-defeating thoughts and turn them into positive thoughts through reframing.

Dialectical Behavior Therapy (DBT) is "a flexible, stage-based therapy that combines principles of behavior therapy, cognitive behavior therapy, and mindfulness. Its underlying emphasis is on helping individuals learn both to regulate and to tolerate their emotions[12]." "DBT is an evidence-based treatment that is derived from CBT. DBT encourages experiencing and accepting the emotions and developing healthy ways to cope with them (Jones 2022)[13]." I still use dialectical behavior therapy, like using a weighted blanket, baking cookies, meditating on Bible verses (all distress tolerance), identifying pros and cons, and focusing on emotional regulation through mindfulness and testing the five senses. DBT has taught me self-awareness and emotion regulation.

One dialectical behavior therapy tool I learned about in the day treatment programs is having a safe place in your mind—a place of escape during times of anxiety and depression. My happy place is to think of being in a rocking chair outside a cabin in the mountains, with my trusty dog and horse with me. I think of the cool wind blowing through my hair. My happy

---

[11] Jones, Heather. Dialectical Behavior Therapy vs. Cognitive Behavioral Therapy. Very Well Health. October 15, 2022. https://www.verywellhealth.com/dialectical-behavior-therapy-vs-cognitive-behavioral-therapy-uses-benefits-side-effects-and-more-5323767

[12] "Dialectical Behavior Therapy." APA Dictionary of Psychology. American Psychological Association, Accessed January 1, 2024. https://dictionary.apa.org/dialectical-behavior-therapy.

[13] Jones, Heather. Dialectical Behavior Therapy vs. Cognitive Behavioral Therapy. Very Well Health. October 15, 2022. https://www.verywellhealth.com/dialectical-behavior-therapy-vs-cognitive-behavioral-therapy-uses-benefits-side-effects-and-more-5323767

place is a welcome distraction from my racing thoughts. Another happy place is at the beach with a book, which is a great way to relax. If your happy places do not work, try baking cookies or placing a warm blanket straight out of the dryer on you. These help to distract me from racing thoughts or the darkness that tries to envelop me.

"Coping mechanisms are behaviors that aim to avoid stress or unpleasant emotions[14]. These behaviors can be positive (adaptive) or negative (maladaptive). Problem-focused coping aims to eliminate or change the source of your stress, while emotion-focused coping helps you change the way you react to your stressors[15]." "Some emotion-focused coping mechanisms would be meditating, practicing mindfulness, exercising, taking a bubble bath, and practicing deep breathing. Some problem-focused coping mechanisms would be seeking therapy, establishing healthy boundaries, improving time management, and being proactive[16]." Since learning about different coping skills like mindfulness (staying in the present time while paying attention to your thoughts, feelings, and sensations without judgment. It helps reduce stress, improve mental well-being, and enhance focus and self-awareness), five senses (grounding technique that lets you experience the five basic human senses: touch, sight, hearing, smell and taste while staying in the present moment), deep breathing (4 inhale–7 hold–8 exhale or 4-4-4), and video-guided meditation (a video of mind-body practice where an experienced teacher walks you through the meditative process and often describes relaxing images and scenarios to set the tone and mood), most of my anxiety has gone away. I practiced five senses until I could stop dissociating

---

[14] "Coping Mechanism." APA Dictionary of Psychology. American Psychological Association, Accessed January 1, 2024. https://dictionary.apa.org/coping-mechanism.

[15] Bailey, Aubrey. "Coping Mechanisms: Everything You Need to Know." Very Well Health. January 1, 2024. https://www.verywellhealth.com/coping-mechanisms-5272135.

[16] Bailey, Aubrey. "Coping Mechanisms: Everything You Need to Know." Very Well Health. January 1, 2024. https://www.verywellhealth.com/coping-mechanisms-5272135.

(like an out of body experience), a significant problem in my life. I did this by tasting mints, hot chocolate, and tea, smelling lit candles, feeling the weighted blanket wrapped around me, looking at photos, or listening to classical music. I also snap my fingers near my ears to keep me grounded and use the dive reflex, which is when I splash water on my face. Sometimes, I use counting backward from 100 in 3s or 7s to ground myself mentally. With these tools and my medications, my nightmares and flashbacks are getting better. I sit in a rocking chair outside before bed and practice deep breathing exercises for about 2-3 minutes at night. That also calms me and puts me to sleep.Have you ever stopped to sit outside and watch the sunset or simply smell the roses? Nature truly is God's gift to us. God tells us through creation that He loves us all day long. Here is my greatest coping mechanism: One thing I love doing is walking in my neighborhood and talking to God while doing it. He is the God of all comfort. He will never leave you nor forsake you. Praying is simple, yet as human beings, we make it hard. I tell Him everything about my day, like how I feel and how my day went. I praise Him, thank Him for all He has done, and then ask for what I need. A local Bible study taught me to ask, seek, and knock with the good Lord daily. He is easy to talk to and loves you a lot. Before walks with God, I can still remember the walks around the neighborhood with my mom. She would check in with me and talk about how our days went. We would laugh and sometimes cry, making the time and distance go quickly.

    I also like to call a friend or talk to someone. I used to have trouble making friends and isolated myself constantly since I felt socially awkward. Then, one day, I started looking for things in common with others. I would search online for local groups and then make myself go. At first, I would not say anything, but as time passed, I grew close enough to share about myself. Today, many friends love me unconditionally and support me when needed. Peer connection and community support have helped me end my social isolation and loneliness. However, my diagnosis can reduce social drive and contact when my symptoms are heightened. I encourage you to always ask for help and support when y'all need it.

With my mental health, sometimes I am socially awkward. So, I started looking for a way to start conversations and express myself artistically. I recently decided to put stickers on my car. I have places I have been to, Dachshund stickers, Christian stickers, sports decals, Star Wars stickers, and Marvel stickers. I have had people comment on them and start a conversation that I would have struggled to have otherwise. Praise God! Thank you to the people who engage and encourage me to have conversations!

My most recent thing to do is listen to worship music out loud as I walk. It is also a conversation starter. People say they like my worship music, and others have thanked me. What a miracle! I can praise God and preach the Gospel while walking and worshipping!

One of my greatest coping mechanisms is practicing the Sabbath, which does not have to be on Sunday, and I can make it any day of the week when I am free. My most significant need is intimacy with God. I am stuck more in the how versus why now. I long to spend time with my Abba. I talk to God like anybody else and rest in Him. I want to walk and talk with Him. I enjoy going on walks and praying. My Sabbath should be spent relaxing with God. Maybe this year, I will finish reading the New Testament of the Bible. Perhaps I can watch more sunsets while thanking God for His creation. I could color Him a picture or paint with beauty. I could fellowship with family over dinner or watch a movie. I could dance to some praise and worship music in my room. Reading my Bible is not a stressor but a delight. Time spent with God is truly precious. A day spent with God is one without care where I can be myself and have fun, where we laugh and love. I wish to share the love my Abba and I have for each other. The joy I have through the good and bad keeps me going. Time spent with my Abba is well spent. The hope I have found in Jesus Christ is everlasting. He died for me and rose to sit at the right hand of God. My adoption as a daughter of the King of Kings excites me. I long to see Him with open arms and a loving heart. I can only imagine climbing into His lap and giving Him a big hug. I get to share eternity with the lover of my soul and my brothers and sisters in Christ. What a happy reunion it will be!

> Step 6 to talking to someone self-injuring:
> **Always extend an open invitation to talk anytime.**

CHAPTER 10

The Importance of Community as a Social Support System

Zephaniah 3:17 "For the Lord your God is living among you. He is a mighty savior. He will take delight in you with gladness. With his love, he will calm all your fears. He will rejoice over you with joyful songs."

The community around you is important when you struggle because "a community can provide us with a sense of belonging, support, and identity. Experiencing a sense of belonging is vital for our psychological well-being. Being a part of a healthy community can help us feel connected to others, as well as feel we're part of something larger than ourselves. This is especially important for people who've experienced trauma or loss, or who are feeling isolated, marginalized, bullied, or alone. For those, and for all of us, a community can provide that necessary sense of belonging. Being a part of a healthy community can also provide us with support. When we're going through a difficult time, it can be enormously helpful to have people who we can turn to. Community members can offer us emotional support, practical help, and advice. They can also help us to feel we aren't alone in our struggles. A community can also help us to develop a sense of identity. When we're part of a community, we learn about shared values and beliefs. We also

The Importance of Community as a Social Support System

learn about our history and culture. This can help us feel we have a place in the world, and that we are part of something important (Stein 2023)[17]."

The best thing the community can do for a patient is to be there for them by listening to them, asking how they are doing or just checking in on them with your full attention, being compassionate while helping them, asking if they need prayer, allowing them to volunteer when they can because it gives a sense of purpose, and giving physical touch, like a giving a hug, holding a hand, or putting an arm around them, which can make them feel supported and cared for during a challenging time. Remember: prayer, care, and share because showing up for the people we care about matters to them, but make sure you remain present throughout and after their crisis, which is important. Sometimes, we just need a friend. If they are in the hospital, please visit and sit with them, or pick up the phone and give them a call. Sometimes, they won't be able to verbalize their feelings, wants, or needs. By telling them and showing them that you care, you are loving them in words and actions. After all, during a difficult time, they need all the love they can get.

In my community, I have a psychiatrist, whom I have worked with since middle school, a counselor who teaches me new things about my illness and growth, family and friends, who build me up and encourage me, and my church family, who are there praying the whole way. I need prayers, meal trains, care packages, and Jesus Christ. Jesus Christ is the Great Comforter. He has been there with me every step of the way. He has felt my pain and walked through this life with me. I am not talking about religion but a relationship with Jesus Christ, God's Son and the Messiah. Through my counselor, Jesus Christ is teaching me healthy boundaries and balance. My family, including church members, also celebrate the small steps with me,

---

[17] Stein, Samantha. The Importance of Community. Psychology Today. July 18, 2023. https://www.psychologytoday.com/us/blog/what-the-wild-things-are/202307/the-importance-of-community

sometimes moment by moment. My community sees me as a person and a child of God, not my illness.

A client should find a counselor, trusted friend, or family member for inspiration and accountability. If you want to grow, bring encouraging people around you. Life is about the quality of friends, not quantity. I personally seek deep connection, mutual support, and true companionship. Life also lets go of people who are not supposed to be in your life. There should be balance and healthy boundaries in all your relationships. Establishing and maintaining boundaries are setting healthy boundaries (a psychological demarcation that protects the integrity of an individual or group or that helps the person or group set realistic limits on participation in a relationship or activity[18]) that help protect your mental and emotional health.

Friends and family are my greatest support systems. They may not completely understand what I go through, but they empathize with me and have compassion for my situation. Oftentimes, people do not really understand that my life is different or that I struggle even though I look perfectly fine. While most people have been happy to accommodate my needs when I am struggling, sometimes it is still hard for them to understand. It does not mean that they do not care, but they may not know how to help or that you even need support. So, tell them what is happening in your life and let them listen to you. Life is always worth fighting for, and it is hard to fight alone.

I have to brag about my small group at church for a minute. My friends create a safe place to talk where I can laugh, smile, and cry with them. I have a voice, and they encourage and lift me up. I have found that I can process, think, and just be, which makes all the difference. I can be honest without fear or judgment. I genuinely trust again. With their support, I can cry out to God and let others help me while growing stronger relationships and

---

[18] "Boundary." APA Dictionary of Psychology. American Psychological Association, Accessed January 1, 2024. https://dictionary.apa.org/boundary.

spiritual roots. I need fellowship, hugs, and to share my pain. With their support, I can lament to God and allow Jesus Christ to heal my broken heart. Fear had paralyzed me, but now I have learned to love and trust again. Rick Warren once said, "The greater the grief, the fewer words needed." This rings true in my daily life. In Joel Comiskey's article on the early church, he talks about Paul wanting believers to become "witnesses through their words, lives, and suffering, by encouraging each other, sharing transparently, and rejoicing in God's goodness (Comiskey 2023)[19]." Our small group reminds me of *Colossians 3:16* when it says, *"Let the word of Christ dwell in you richly as you teach and admonish one another with all wisdom, and as you sing psalms, hymns, and spiritual songs with gratitude in your hearts to God."*

You can gain strength and encouragement when you spend time with your Christian sisters. Share with them your struggles so they can have care, compassion, and prayer for the situation. In return, help them have faith and grow in Christlikeness.

The next two paragraphs are dedicated to the family and community at large: Small acts of kindness and gratitude can go a long way. Write a thank you card to make people feel seen, appreciated, and understood. Thank them for the things they do or for who they are. Remind them of their worth as a child of God and that they are never alone. Please, let them know that you are there for them or thinking about them. By doing this, you are being thoughtful. If they do not answer right away or show signs of improvement, that is okay. Simple text messages or phone calls also work. Also, consider a prayer chain for them as a powerful symbol of the support all around them.

Care packages or thoughtful gifts are excellent too. Consider something practical or useful, or maybe something that reminds them of a more

---

[19] Comiskey, Joel. "What Was the New Testament Church Like?" Christianity Today. Retrieved January 1, 2023, from https://www.smallgroups.com/articles/2015/what-was-new-testament-church-like.html

positive time in their lives. You could put in a coloring book with colored pencils, some snacks they like, a paint-by-numbers, a thank you card or note of encouragement, the music they want, or a gift card to a great restaurant nearby. These can be good reminders that they are loved. Please keep it simple and fun. Surprises can make a person joyful.

> Step 7 to talking to someone self-injuring: **Once you listen and offer support and caring, the best way to help is to get your friend to a responsible mental health professional. They can help them stop the behavior and learn new coping mechanisms.**

CHAPTER 11

The Struggles of Work

Jeremiah 29:11-13 "For I know the plans I have for you," says the Lord. "They are plans for good and not for disaster, to give you a future and a hope. In those days when you pray, I will listen. If you look for me wholeheartedly, you will find me."

I started college in 2003 and took fourteen years to complete my first bachelor's degree. I did only a few courses at a time and took off the summers to recuperate. I frequently saw a counselor and had a community of people who rallied around me.

After going to a local college in San Antonio, my family and I moved from South Texas to North Texas. I struggled to have the energy and strength to work a job. Although I had a degree, I needed help with numbers, and frequently read them backwards. A cashier job would not work, so I volunteered at the local food pantry. I do believe volunteering helps create gratitude and, in turn, happiness. I enjoyed stocking the shelves, bagging groceries, and loading cars with groceries. I felt a sense of purpose. I got to practice my social skills while there and made some friends. If you have a mental illness, you know this can be hard. I was eager to learn but had lots of questions. I would frequently forget where things went or would have to ask what to do next. The staff was always patient with me. They would keep encouraging me to come back. I learned some valuable lessons here that help with my mental illness. I encourage you to practice generosity with your time, energy, and money. Giving is better than receiving (Acts 20:35, Luke 6:38, Malachi 3:10).

It took me nearly two decades before I found a great job that understood me. In 2021, I decided to pursue a working career. My medications were in order, I had a community around me, and I had a God who orchestrated the events. I applied to be a team member at a local restaurant. I quickly failed at the cash register and asked my boss if I could be the dishwasher. I excelled there. Sometimes there was pressure to hurry, but I managed to get things done. After a hostile work environment incident, I left the company. I took a few months off, then switched to a different field with a company I have now left. I loved my job and was promoted within four months on the job. I had to leave due to an incident that negatively impacted my mental health.

It is okay if you struggle with working, and it does not mean you are less of a person because of it. I can only work part-time if I do work, which is not right now. I understand if you cannot or will not, and I am struggling with this more as I get older.

I am considered my version of high-functioning today. I can work part-time and go about my day smiling while accepting what is happening inside. It does not mean my life is symptom-free. Lingering symptoms, for me, frequently occur while taking medications. I have depression, mania, and intense anxiety during this time. I see the psychiatrist regularly with trips to the pharmacy and handfuls of pills every day. I knew that my life would never be the same. I am just thankful that my treatment works as well as it does. I did not have hallucinations or delusions from 2012 through 2023.

I have experienced housing and employment discrimination. My mental illness often prevents me from working. I have tried getting a job but was turned down because I mentioned my mental health concerns. I recommend only talking with the human resources department after you pass the first few rounds of interviews. I recommend practicing staying calm and saying, "Thank you for the opportunity, and have a nice day." Due to my illness preventing me from working, I faced prejudice and felt shame from a loved one due to this. They did not believe in psychiatrists and thought that I should not discuss my mental illness. They said that I should not show weakness and that my emotions and asking for help are a sign of weakness. They are a perfectionist and a workaholic who thought I should work harder and study and focus on school or getting a job. I no longer have contact with this person. Regarding housing discrimination, there are not enough Section 8 housing for people with mental health concerns and long wait lists. I recommend planning at least three years in advance.

I do want to commend my mom, who saw me struggling and got me the help I needed. She went with me to my psychiatric appointments to share my blind spots. She has been more receptive to talking about what she has gone through. With her my psychiatric appointments have been about being open, honest, humble, and graceful. My treatment plan has become a collaboration between my care team and me.

Nevertheless, enough about what I have survived. What about what I do for volunteer work? I volunteer at Meals on Wheels some mornings when I am needed, the Women's Center Rape Crisis Unit usually three or four times a month, Friends of Lancaster Homeless Ministry once a month, Operation Christmas Child every fall, Regeneration throughout the year, and Hope Ministries, where I lead a support group for those living with mental illnesses. That does not include the people I take care of, like a friend of mine, who is elderly and I visit once a week, or my friends who go through their own depression and anxiety on a regular basis. Funny thing: It really does take a community to survive. Our lives are so entwined that we take care of each other regularly. You have to lift each other up daily. Currently,

I am going back to college for a degree in social work. While in college, I want to be pushed out of my comfort zone and try new things, especially through volunteering and internships. I am looking forward to my variety of classes. Right now, I am looking at becoming a Licensed Clinical Social Worker in the mental health field and working at a local food pantry, rape crisis center, or domestic violence women's shelter. I absolutely love helping others and feel like social work is my calling, especially with people who have faced similar experiences. The volunteer work and college give me a sense of purpose and a reason to live.

> Step 8 to talking to someone self-injuring:
> **Point out their strengths**.

PART 3
Where My Faith Comes Alive

CHAPTER 12

Compassion: A Call to Action

Proverbs 31:20 *"She extends a helping hand to the poor and opens her arms to the needy."*

Have you ever wondered what compassion actually means? According to Dictionary.com[20], the definition of compassion is "a feeling of deep sympathy and sorrow for another who is stricken by misfortune, accompanied by a strong desire to alleviate the suffering." It is more than just an emotion. It is emotion plus action, in word and deed. It gives you an insight into another's need and it enables you to understand their hurts. I believe compassion is people helping people out of a genuine sense of caring. It comes from your heart and ultimately God. Remember, the ultimate example of compassion was God sending His one and only Son to die for you and me on the cross (John 3:16-17).

The world is crying out to us in desperation for help. According to the World Bank, almost 700 million people worldwide live today in extreme poverty, while living on less than $2.15 per a day which is the extreme poverty line (World Bank 2023)[21]. On top of that, there is homelessness, child

---

[20] "Compassion." Dictionary.com. Accessed January 1, 2024. https://www.dictionary.com/browse/compassion.

[21] World Bank. "World Bank Group–International Development, Poverty, & Sustainability," 2023. https://www.worldbank.org/en/home.

labor, abuse, slavery, sexual exploitation, AIDS and other illnesses, war, natural disasters, and much more. Time and time again people just read these words and do not engage their hearts. Imagine if those people who were hurting were in your family and community. Would your attitude be different? The Lord wants us to take them into our hearts and make them family. After all, we are all His children, who are made in His image.

How can you make a difference? I believe that everyone can do something simple every day, such as smiling at a stranger, helping an elderly neighbor, counseling a friend, making a donation to charity, or simply lending a hand.

Here are some personal examples of compassion:

I used to volunteer every Thursday evening at the Children's Shelter with other college students from a local church. There was a particular Thursday that I remember well. We arrived at 6:15 pm. When we went to greet the kids, one of the older kids ran up to me and gave me a giant bear hug and said she missed me. Then I went and played with the toddlers for about an hour. Puzzles, games, and dance-dance-revolution—the toddler way—filled my evening. Then it was time for the toddlers to hit the showers. This little toddler hugged me and so I responded that I would see her soon. Then I went to play with the energetic, big kids. We played basketball, soccer, and other games. When 8 pm rolled around, it was time to go and I was sad. After signing out, a girl ran up to me. This little girl gave me a huge hug and said, "I don't know you, but I love you!" As my eyes filled with tears, I reminded myself that everything was going to be okay because it was in God's hands. I said, upon being asked why I volunteer there, "I am the glimpse of hope in the child's eyes when all is lost." I am not sure who helped who more, but I will always remember it.

I used to volunteer at Assault Victim Services in San Angelo. Having clocked in more than 270 hours, I experienced more than I could ever imagine. Long nights were spent working the hotline and going on hospital visits. But it was definitely all worth it. Imagine getting to the hospital because a thirteen or fourteen-year-old girl had been sexually assaulted. She looks you in the eyes and says she is scared, but you are too. However, you have to be the strong one. You sit there all night holding her cold hands and keep whispering that everything will be alright. In the morning, you leave knowing you will never see each other again, but you share a deep connection that will last a lifetime.

My social worker, who guides me, confirmed my perception of the social work profession and gave me some excitement for my career. She inspired me to volunteer at the Women's Center as a rape crisis victim advocate. While there, I learned about visiting rape crisis victims in the hospital and listening to hotline calls. I learned that social work is hard work but very rewarding. I had the opportunity to do four hospital visits and two hotline calls recently. I realized that I have a heart for rape crisis victims and possibly want to work with them as a social worker someday. I was the victim's support during hospital visits and also handed out clothing and packets of information to victims. The hardest part was being in the hospital room for the sexual assault exam and holding the hand of the lady while trying to comfort her. I started in October 2023, and will continue to volunteer here for the future.

My current social worker is absolutely right, "A small act of kindness, a few encouraging words, and just letting someone know help is out there, can make a big difference. It can be the lifeline that pulls them back from the edge."

CHAPTER 13

I Want to Be like Jesus, David, Paul, Mary, and Ruth...

Matthew 5: 14-16 "You are the light of the world–like a city on a hilltop that cannot be hidden. No one lights a lamp and then puts it under a basket. Instead, a lamp is placed on a stand, where it gives light to everyone in the house. In the same way, let your good deeds shine out for all to see, so that everyone will praise your heavenly Father."

As I read the Bible this year, I have dreamed of being a unique person of faith. I want to live like the believers in the hall of faith (Hebrews 11). Faith is confident hope in knowing that God's promises will be fulfilled. I want to hold onto God's promises like Sarah, be fervent in prayer like Hannah, have the anointing of a judge like Deborah, have the courage to change like Rahab, be a wise and humble servant leader like Ruth, have the courage to trust and believe God like Mary (Jesus' mother), serve Jesus Christ like Mary Magdalene, have a heart after God like David, and have courage and humility with all my trials and tribulations like Paul. But most of all, I want to have the compassion, empathy, love, sacrifice, and patience of my Jesus Christ. The unchangeable and perfect character of God is amazing. But a huge fear in my life has been not living up to my potential as a child of

God. I want to help others, hope when it is impossible, care for the unreachable, find joy in trials, persevere through tribulations, forgive the unforgivable, pray for all people, have patience with and love for my enemies, and have faith that moves mountains. The days I live for God, where I ignore the busyness of life, crawl onto my Abba's (God the Father's) lap and lay my head against His shoulders for rest and peace, or days when I disregard my need inorder to fulfill someone else's needs, those are the days where I truly live. May I have the faith and perseverance that reminds others of my Lord and Savior Jesus Christ, who is my hero. And maybe when I get to Heaven, I will hear my Lord and Savior say, "Well done, good and faithful servant!"

CHAPTER 14

Helping You Become a Child of God... a Personal Decision to Follow Christ

All the broken, wounded, weary, and lonely can find hope, love, and strength in the Savior's arms. If you're lost, hurting, and feeling all alone, there's hope that is calling, so come and find your home. We have had highs and lows, but through it all, we are children of God and are safe in our Father's arms. So come running to our Father because He is waiting with open arms. He even meets the prodigals and older sisters like me. I wouldn't be here without Jesus Christ. If God hadn't sent His one and only Son to die for me and all people who accept Him as Savior and Lord, I would be lost in a world of turmoil. Jesus Christ reconciled the lost to God. Pure chaos runs this world, as it is ruled by Satan, but if I can just light the way for one person at a time, I will have done my job. Grace is truly an amazing thing once you realize that we are saved by grace through faith in Jesus Christ and not by works. We are created for good works, not saved by good works. Being a child of God is one of the most humbling things. Nothing compares to being a child of God, who loves us unconditionally. I am adopted, chosen, and loved unconditionally because of Jesus Christ, God's Son, and my Lord and Savior. I am even co-heir with Christ and will see an inheritance in Heaven. I did not earn it or deserve it. My salvation is only by Jesus Christ's birth, life, death, resurrection, and ascension. He took all my sins (humans are sinful by nature, which simply means missing God's mark), casting them as far as the east is from the west (Psalms 103:12), washing me white as snow (Isaiah 1:18). Jesus Christ grants forgiveness of sin and eternal life when sinners repent and profess their faith in Him alone. I am genuinely in love with God, who is eternal, omniscient, omnipotent, and for all He has done and will continue to do. You, too, can become a child of God by making a personal decision to follow Jesus Christ (Acts 4:12). Have a conversation (prayer) with God. It is like talking to anyone else, but He responds when you repent (turn away from sin) of your sins by sending the Holy Spirit into your heart. You may not feel any different. It is based on God's promise that you will be saved if you make the decision to follow Jesus Christ and believe in Him as your Lord and Savior. We are officially saved as soon as we make a personal decision to follow Christ, and we can know for sure that we are going to Heaven. You will want to share this with others. Remember, once a Christian, God speaks to us through a still small voice in your heart or through other Christians. Congratulations on becoming a child of God! Now trust and obey the good Lord. Life's purpose is knowing, loving, and serving God with all one's heart, mind, strength, and soul. The Bible is accurate, reliable, and always relevant. God Bless!

Consider the blessing of being in a relationship with the Creator of the Universe—the blessing of being able to serve Him, which yields an abundance of joy and purpose. Draw close to the One who loves you unconditionally, and you receive all the comfort and encouragement you need from Him. The Lord is good, always forgiving, and His mercies are new every morning. God's grace brings peace, hope, and healing. Whenever you stumble, He will pick you up with open arms. His love was evident on the cross and is indescribable, immeasurable, and unshakable. The God of the universe, who numbers the hairs on your head, is invested in His relationship with you. Your relationship with Him, which you will work on building and strengthening for the rest of your life, is a place where you can be known and loved. Have confidence in His love for you; you should nurture your hope in Him for all eternity.

God has a plan for you, a plan to give you a future and a hope. Walk in the truth of His promises and entrust your future to Him. He wants to use you for His glory; seek His guidance with your time, talents, and energy. You can come to Him with your concerns, dreams, hurts, and desires. God will empower you to seek to live out His will, to love Him, and to love others. Run to Him whenever you face difficult decisions or challenging circumstances. Diligently seek Him.

CHAPTER 15
Healing Rain

Sometimes, relationships come hard for me due to my mental illness, but my friends pull me from the mess I am in when we meet. Sometimes, I just have to stop and trust them. They are right. At the cross, I am forgiven, saved, and loved beyond a shadow of a doubt. God loves me, so I should love myself! Now, I am moving on because the best investment I can make is in myself. Now, it is time to adapt and overcome.

As I try to sort out my feelings about letting my relationship with my biological father go, I grieve about the loss but grow closer together with my mom in love and compassion. I realize that I am not a lost cause anymore, but still struggle to learn how to love again. So, my counselor teaches me how to live again by recognizing my strengths, passions, and capabilities. Sometimes, I need help to tap into my sense of empowerment and fight for what I believe in. I feel so much better after releasing the pain of all my trauma. I need to start setting boundaries because I am not the problem and it is not my fault. So, how do I forgive my father and other men in my life for the abuse and alcoholism? How did I find hope in the situation when there was absolutely none left? For me, it started with finding Jesus Christ. How do I end the cycle of abuse without hurting them or me? I released it. I said it out loud without judging myself and learned to love, empathize, and have compassion for myself. I recognized that I am loving, caring, and generous. So, as I long to start my master's degree, I hope to help others see who they are in Christ, as my friends and counselors have shown me. Who knows, maybe I will get my PhD in how to help others survive mental illness, especially Schizoaffective Disorder, or how to prevent it in the first place. The Lord knows that I am more than capable and will provide the way and means.

So, maybe I slept in a closet growing up. I knew no different. The lack of supervision and abandonment did not destroy me. So, there was parentification and terrible abuse and neglect, but I made it out alive. So, was it creepy when my dad watched me sleep? The emotional incest and covert sexual abuse were bad and the emotional abuse was the worst. I do not deny that. Somewhere in the self-hate and doubting myself, I see that I can move forward with courage. I have a choice to do it without forgetting what was behind me because I cannot. Now, I have love and care from family and friends who try to understand me and where I come from. I can use everything as a stepping stone in my time on Earth. After all, we only have one life.

Did the spiritual abuse drown me? No, because God, himself, pursued me back home to himself. He loves me and would never hurt me. So, as I go into the next chapter of my life, I will take what I have learned and pass it on. As a compliant people pleaser, it would do good to remember that brainwashing does not end you. So, is there hope once again? Yes, Christ died on the cross for us and comforts us in our toughest and lowest times. So yeah, I used to carve words into my arms that I believed. However, God rescued me, and I do not have to have it all together for Him, but I can rely on Him to get me through with sustaining grace. My disorder draws me closer to God with more dependency on him. I have not been completely healed, but I believe I will be in Heaven. It may not be during this lifetime, but I will pray for it and ask others to pray for me to be completely healed. The anticipation of Heaven and the love and care that God has for me keep me going. Now, I am lovable, compassionate, and an encourager. Do I want to give up anymore? No, I want to make a difference in the lives of others and help them see who they are in Christ and their potential. Yes, I have accepted responsibility for myself and my past, but I am no longer dysfunctional. Maybe I was not sick after all. Maybe it was just the gaslighting and shaming. I am no longer imprisoned within myself or trapped in my own life. So, who am I? I am a child of God and beloved of Christ, absolutely holy and dearly loved...and so are you! Beat that, Sigmund Freud!

I have provided sections on who we are in Christ, encouraging verses, important websites and phone numbers in the resource section and more about myself in the appendixes with my testimony, prayers, and acknowledgments. I hope this helps. Best wishes!

Resources

Characteristics of Who We Are In Christ

Always Loved – 1 John 4:10 "This is real love—not that we loved God, but that he loved us and sent his Son as a sacrifice to take away our sins."

Ephesians 3:17-19 "Then Christ will make his home in your hearts as you trust in him. Your roots will grow down into God's love and keep you strong. And may you have the power to understand, as all God's people should, how wide, how long, how high, and how deep his love is. May you experience the love of Christ, though it is too great to understand fully. Then you will be made complete with all the fullness of life and power that comes from God."

Amazing – Psalm 139:14 "Thank you for making me so wonderfully complex! Your workmanship is marvelous—how well I know it."

Ambassador – 2 Corinthians 5:20 "So we are Christ's ambassadors; God is making his appeal through us. We speak for Christ when we plead, 'Come back to God!'"

Beautiful – Ecclesiastes 3:11 "Yet God has made everything beautiful for its own time. He has planted eternity in the human heart, but even so, people cannot see the whole scope of God's work from beginning to end."

Capable – Mark 10:27 "Jesus looked at them intently and said, 'Humanly speaking, it is impossible. But not with God. Everything is possible with God.'"

Chosen – 1 Peter 2:9 "But you are not like that, for you are a chosen people. You are royal priests, a holy nation, God's very own possession. As a result, you can show others the goodness of God, for he called you out of the darkness into his wonderful light."

Colossians 3:12 "Since God chose you to be the holy people he loves, you must clothe yourselves with tenderhearted mercy, kindness, humility, gentleness, and patience."

John 15:16-17 "You did not choose me. I chose you. I appointed you to go and produce lasting fruit so that the Father will give you whatever you ask for, using my name. This is my command: Love each other."

Created – Genesis 1:27 "So God created human beings in his own image. In the image of God, he created them; male and female he created them."

Ephesians 2:10 "For we are God's masterpiece. He has created us anew in Christ Jesus, so we can do the good things he planned for us long ago."

2 Corinthians 5:17 "This means that anyone who belongs to Christ has become a new person. The old life is gone; a new life has begun!"

Enough – 2 Corinthians 12:9 "Each time he said, 'My grace is all you need. My power works best in weakness.' So now I am glad to boast about my weaknesses so that the power of Christ can work through me."

Forever Free – John 8:36 "So if the Son sets you free, you are truly free."

Forgiveness–Psalm 130:4 "But you offer forgiveness, that we might learn to fear you."

Luke 1:77 "You will tell God's people how to find salvation through forgiveness of their sins."

Acts 13:38 "Brothers, listen! We are here to proclaim that through this man, Jesus, there is forgiveness for your sins."

Colossians 1:13-14 "For God has rescued us from the kingdom of darkness and transferred us into the Kingdom of his dear Son, who purchased our freedom and forgave our sins."

God's Workmanship – Ephesians 2:10 "For we are God's masterpiece. He has created us anew in Christ Jesus, so we can do the good things he planned for us long ago."

Helped–Psalm 121:1-2 "I look up to the mountains–does my help come from there? My help comes from the Lord, who made heaven and earth!"

Joint Heir – Romans 8:17 "And since we are his children, we are his heirs. In fact, together with Christ we are heirs of God's glory. But if we are to share his glory, we must also share his suffering."

Never Alone – Matthew 28:20 "Teach these new disciples to obey all the commands I have given you. And be sure of this: I am with you always, even to the end of the age."

Characteristics of Who We Are In Christ

Strong – Philippians 4:13 "For I can do everything through Christ, who gives me strength."

Transformed – Galatians 2:20 "My old self has been crucified with Christ. It is no longer I who live, but Christ lives in me. So I live in this earthly body by trusting in the Son of God, who loved me and gave himself for me."

1 Peter 1:23 "For you have been born again, but not to a life that will quickly end. Your new life will last forever because it comes from the eternal, living word of God."

Romans 12:2 "Don't copy the behavior and customs of this world, but let God transform you into a new person by changing the way you think. Then you will learn to know God's will for you, which is good and pleasing and perfect."

Victorious – Romans 8:37 "No, despite all these things, overwhelming victory is ours through Christ, who loved us."

Encouraging Verses from the Bible

Psalm 82:3-4 "Give justice to the poor and the orphan; uphold the rights of the oppressed and the destitute. Rescue the poor and helpless; deliver them from the grasp of evil people."

Jonah 2:8-9 "Those who worship false gods turn their backs on all God's mercies. But I will offer sacrifices to God with songs of praise, and I will fulfill all my vows. For my salvation comes from the Lord alone."

Matthew 5:3-10 "God blesses those who are poor and realize their need for him, for the Kingdom of Heaven is theirs. God blesses those who mourn, for they will be comforted. God blesses those who are humble, for they will inherit the whole earth. God blesses those who hunger and thirst for justice, for they will be satisfied. God blesses those who are merciful, for they will be shown mercy. God blesses those whose hearts are pure, for they will see God. God blesses those who work for peace, for they will be called the children of God. God blesses those who are persecuted for doing right, for the Kingdom of Heaven is theirs."

Matthew 5: 11-12 "God blesses you when people mock you and persecute you and lie about you and say all sorts of evil things against you because you are my followers. Be happy about it! Be very glad! For a great reward awaits you in heaven. And remember, the ancient prophets were persecuted in the same way."

Matthew 11:28 "Then Jesus said, 'Come to me, all of you who are weary and carry heavy burdens, and I will give you rest.'"

Matthew 18:3-4 "Then he said, 'I tell you the truth, unless you turn from your sins and become like little children, you will never get into the Kingdom of Heaven. So anyone who becomes as humble as this little child is the greatest in the Kingdom of Heaven.'"

Mark 9:36-37 "Then he put a little child among them. Taking the child in his arms, he said to them, 'Anyone who welcomes a little child like this on my behalf welcomes me, and anyone who welcomes me welcomes not only me but also my Father who sent me.'"

Luke 6:27-28, 35-36 "But to you who are willing to listen, I say, love your enemies! Do good to those who hate you. Bless those who curse you. Pray for those who hurt you. Love your enemies! Do good to them. Lend to them without expecting to be repaid. Then your reward from heaven will be very great, and you will truly be acting as children of the Most High, for he is kind to those who are unthankful and wicked. You must be compassionate, just as your Father is compassionate."

Romans 3:23-26 "For everyone has sinned; we all fall short of God's glorious standard. Yet God, in his grace, freely makes us right in his sight. He did this through Christ Jesus when he freed us from the penalty for our sins. For God presented Jesus as the sacrifice for sin. People are made right with God when they believe that Jesus sacrificed his life, shedding his blood.

This sacrifice shows that God was being fair when he held back and did not punish those who sinned in times past, for he was looking ahead and including them in what he would do in this present time. God did this to demonstrate his righteousness, for he himself is fair and just, and he makes sinners right in his sight when they believe in Jesus."

2 Corinthians 5:7 "For we live by believing and not by seeing."

Galatians 5:22-23 "But the Holy Spirit produces this kind of fruit in our lives: love, joy, peace, patience, kindness, goodness, faithfulness, gentleness, and self-control. There is no law against these things!"

Ephesians 4:2-3 "Always be humble and gentle. Be patient with each other, making allowance for each other's faults because of your love. Make every effort to keep yourselves united in the Spirit, binding yourselves together with peace."

Ephesians 5:1-2 "Imitate God, therefore, in everything you do, because you are his dear children. Live a life filled with love, following the example of Christ. He loved us and offered himself as a sacrifice for us, a pleasing aroma to God."

Ephesians 5:15-20 "So be careful how you live. Don't live like fools, but like those who are wise. Make the most of every opportunity in these evil days. Don't act thoughtlessly, but understand what the Lord wants you to do. Don't be drunk with wine, because that will ruin your life. Instead, be filled with the Holy Spirit, singing psalms and hymns and spiritual songs among yourselves, and making music to the Lord in your hearts. And give thanks for everything to God the Father in the name of our Lord Jesus Christ."

Philippians 4:8 "And now, dear brothers and sisters, one final thing. Fix your thoughts on what is true, and honorable, and right, and pure, and lovely, and admirable. Think about things that are excellent and worthy of praise."

Revelation 1:4-8 "This letter is from John to the seven churches in the province of Asia. 'Grace and peace to you from the one who is, who always was, and who is still to come; from the sevenfold Spirit before his throne; and from Jesus Christ. He is the faithful witness to these things, the first to rise from the dead, and the ruler of all the kings of the world. All glory to him who loves us and has freed us from our sins by shedding his blood for us. He has made us a Kingdom of priests for God his Father. All glory and power to him forever and ever! Amen. Look! He comes with the clouds of heaven. And everyone will see him–even those who pierced him. And all the nations of the world will mourn for him. Yes! Amen! 'I am the Alpha and the Omega–the beginning and the end,' says the Lord God. 'I am the one who is, who always was, and who is still to come–the Almighty One.'"

Revelation 19:1-2, 6-7 "After this, I heard what sounded like a vast crowd in heaven shouting, 'Praise the Lord! Salvation and glory and power belong to our God. His judgments are true and just.' Then I heard again what sounded like the shout of a vast crowd or the roar of mighty ocean waves or the crash of loud thunder: 'Praise the Lord! For the Lord our God, the Almighty, reigns. Let us be glad and rejoice, and let us give honor to him.' Then the twenty-four elders and the four living beings fell down and worshiped God, who was sitting on the throne. They cried out, 'Amen! Praise the Lord!" And from the throne came a voice that said, "Praise our God, all his servants, all who fear him, from the least to the greatest.'"

"Treasure Box" or "Emergency Toolbox" Example

Books:

- "God Thinks You're Wonderful!" by Max Lucado
- "Bible Promises for You"
- 3:16 New Testament with Psalms and Proverbs
- Favorite book or devotional
- Book for Dummies on Favorite Hobby (learning/teaching book)
- Small booklet on Easter Reflections
- "Reclaiming the Lost Art of Biblical Meditation" by Robert J. Morgan

Worksheets:

- Pamphlets on mental health from NAMI
- Keys/Steps to Managing Stress Worksheet
- Phone List in Case of Emergency
- Coping Skills Worksheet
- Wellness and Relapse Prevention Plan

Personal Letters, etc.

- Personal Testimony Typed Out
- Photos of Family and Friends
- Granny's Obituary After Death
- Letter Written to Self while in Hospital
- Get Well/Birthday Cards

Art Therapy:

- Anti-stress art therapy adult coloring books
- Crayons, Colored Pencils (Plus Sharpener), Pens, Highlighters, Gel Pens
- Paint-by-numbers

Others:

- Spiral notebook for journaling
- Gratitude Journal
- Word Search Books
- "Who I Am in Christ" spiral
- Colored Slinky
- Favorite Music for Every Emotion (mostly Christian)
- "The Chosen" Series on Blu-ray
- Stuffed Animal
- Fuzzy Socks
- Favorite Hard Candy (like Jolly Ranchers)

Struggling and Needing Resources?

If you or someone you know is struggling, do not hesitate to ask for help! You are not alone!

Here are some helpful Mental Health Resources:

LOCAL RESOURCES

Finding Help in Texas: https://www.211texas.org/

Here for Texas–Mental Health Resources for Texas: https://www.herefortexas.com/

Grant Haliburton Foundation: https://www.granthalliburton.org/

United Way of Metropolitan Dallas: https://unitedwaydallas.org/

United Way of Tarrant County: https://www.unitedwaytarrant.org/

Mental Health Association of Greater Dallas: https://mhadallas.org/

National Alliance on Mental Illness (NAMI) Dallas: https://www.naminorthtexas.org/

Struggling and Needing Resources?

National Alliance on Mental Illness (NAMI) Tarrant County: https://namitarrant.org/

SELF HELP RESOURCES

Self-Compassion: https://self-compassion.org/

GET HELP NOW

988 Suicide & Crisis Lifeline is a national network of local crisis centers that provides free and confidential emotional support to people in suicidal crisis or emotional distress 24/7.

Dial 988 or https://988lifeline.org/

Crisis Text Line
Crisis Text Line is a free, 24/7 texting service for those in crisis. Every texter is connected with a crisis counselor, a real-life human being trained to bring texters from a hot moment to a cool calm through active listening and collaborative problem solving. The text line is available from anywhere in the U.S.

Text HOME to 741741 or https://www.crisistextline.org/

The Trevor Project
The Trevor Lifeline is an initiative of The Trevor Project, the leading national organization providing crisis intervention and suicide prevention services to lesbian, gay, bisexual, transgender, queer, and questioning youth. Trained counselors are available 24/7/365.
1-866-488-7386 or https://www.thetrevorproject.org/get-help

Resources for Young People

WEBSITES

Teen Talk: https://teentalk.ca/
Teen Talk is a youth health education program. They provide services for youth from a harm reduction, prevention education perspective.

JED Foundation: https://jedfoundation.org/
JED is a nonprofit that exists to protect emotional health and prevent suicide for our nation's teens and young adults.

Be Vocal : Speak Up for Mental Health: http://www.bevocalspeakup.com/
Be Vocal : Speak Up for Mental Health is an initiative encouraging people across America to use their voice in support of mental health.

Half of US: https://www.mentalhealthishealth.us/
Half of Us aims to initiate a public dialogue to raise awareness about the prevalence of mental health issues and connect students to the appropriate resources to get help.

Foundry: https://foundrybc.ca/
Foundry offers young people ages 12 to 24 health and wellness resources, services, and supports-online and through integrated service centers in seven communities across British Colombia, Canada.

APPS

MindShift App
MindShift is one of the best mental health apps designed specifically for teens and young adults with anxiety.

SuperBetter App
SuperBetter is a game focusing on increasing resilience and the ability to remain strong, optimistic, and motivated when presented with challenging obstacles in life.

MY3 App
MY3 is aimed at those experiencing depression or suicidal thoughts. MY3 asks you to choose three close contacts that you feel comfortable reaching out to when you're down and keeps you connected to this core network.

Rise and Recover App
Rise Up + Recover is a great app for anyone recovering from an eating disorder and wanting to develop a more positive body image.

Calm App
Calm provides people experiencing stress and anxiety with guided meditations, sleep stories, breathing programs, and relaxing music.

Stop, Breathe and Think App
Stop, Breath, and Think helps you check-in with your emotions to receive daily meditation and mindfulness recommendations tuned to how you feel.

Insight Timer App
Insight Timer is the largest free library of guided meditations with more than 20,000 titles available.

Jour App
Jour is a private and portable journaling app for teens and adults. At its core, it is an app that seeks to improve mental health.

Daylio App
Daylio is an easy to use mobile app that allows you to track your moods and daily activities without writing down a single line.

Resources for Parents and Adult Clients:

American Foundation for Suicide Prevention: https://afsp.org/
American Foundation for Suicide Prevention (AFSP) raises awareness, funds scientific research and provides resources and aid to those affected by suicide.

National Institute of Mental Health: https://www.nimh.nih.gov/
National Institute of Mental Health (NIMH) is the lead federal agency for research on mental disorders.

CDC: https://www.cdc.gov/parents/teens/index.html
Centers for Disease Control and Prevention (CDC) is the leading national public health institute of the United States. The CDC is a United States federal agency under the Department of Health and Human Services.

Struggling and Needing Resources?

SAMHSA: https://www.samhsa.gov/
Substance Abuse and Mental Health Services Administration (SAMHSA) is the agency within the U.S. Department of Health and Human Services that leads public health efforts to advance the behavioral health of the nation. SAMHSA's mission is to reduce the impact of substance abuse and mental illness on America's communities.

Mental Health America: https://mhanational.org/
Mental Health America (MHA) – is the nation's leading community-based nonprofit dedicated to addressing the needs of those living with mental illness and to promoting the overall mental health of all Americans.

NAMI: https://www.nami.org/Home
National Alliance on Mental Illness (NAMI) is the nation's largest grassroots mental health organization dedicated to building better lives for the millions of Americans affected by mental illness.

Veteran's Resources:

Veteran's Crisis Hotline:
1-800-273-8255 and Press 1
Text: 838255

Battle Buddy Response Team:
Online: www.battlebuddyresponseteam.org

Stop Soldier Suicide:
Online: www.stopsoldiersuicide.org
Immediate Response: 844-317-1136

Angels With Demons:
Online: www.angelswithdemons.org
Call Out a Veteran Response Team:
855-777-2278

Assistance in Finding Counseling:
Mission 22: www.mission22.com
Give An Hour: www.giveanhour.org
The Elk Institute: www.elkinstitute.us/about-institute

K9 for Warriors:
Service Dog Requests: www.k9sforwarriors.org
Healing Paws for Warriors: www.healingpawsforwarriors.org
Saving Grace K9s: www.savinggracek9s.org

Veterans Helping Veterans:
The Fallen Outdoors: www.thefallenoutdoors.com/get-involved
Giving Back USA–www.givingbackusa.org
The Big Red Barn Retreat–www.thebigredbarnretreat.org

Appendixes

APPENDIX A
If You Knew the Real Me...

I am a child of God, dearly loved and cared for. Someone who is loyal, compassionate, and loving. I don't anger easily and offer abundant mercy and grace. Sometimes I care so much it hurts. I enjoy traveling, listening to worship music, painting, watching sports and Christian shows, collecting sports memorabilia, taking scenic photos, walking in nature, reading Christian books, seeing friends, taking bubble baths, and just breathing and relaxing. I love playing with my dogs and dreaming about rving. I long to be in the mountains or on a beach and Heaven will be the place for me. I love my genealogy and long to travel to the British Isles or maybe even Israel someday. When God tells me I have a hope and future, I believe it even through the storms. My Rock and Salvation will hold me in His right hand. I don't need to worry or fear because He is with me always, loving me moment by moment each day. I am indeed a priest, world changer, disciple maker, and servant leader in a world falling apart. I will not lose hope because I am worthy and loved by the Creator of the Universe, who died to save me. Even if the world falls apart, I will still love Him. That's the real me.

APPENDIX B
My Testimony

I grew up going back and forth between houses as my parents divorced when I was four years old. However, let us not forget that I survived meningitis when I was two and nearly died. Going back and forth was an experience all its own. I had an alcoholic loved one who abused me mentally, emotionally, verbally, physically, sexually, and psychologically. I have survived gaslighting and parental neglect also. I learned to cook and clean at a young age and was content with not being allowed to have friends while I was growing up. The interesting thing is that I thought every household was like mine. I lived in a closet. Sigmund Freud probably would have thrown the book at me a few times. However, that is only a tiny piece of what I have overcome. I survived domestic sexual abuse and spiritual abuse in college, and mental illnesses that nearly killed me. I was told I would never reach my 20s, but I am still here.

While in elementary school and middle school, my mom would drop me off at school early, and I stayed after school for a while. In middle school, I was diagnosed with depression, anxiety, post-traumatic stress disorder, and obsessive-compulsive disorder. I was bullied in school. I had so much shame. I felt sad all the time, and I did not want to do anything. My anxiety was so bad that sometimes, before school, I would throw up due to nerves. I counted and checked everything. On top of that, I had flashbacks of abuse and many nightmares.

High School was awkward, but I searched for a purpose. I loved my English classes best. I always did things backward in Math class, which drove my teachers up the wall. I would eventually get credit for College Algebra by taking a test and for AP English classes.

I did sports in school, which I mostly enjoyed. I played basketball until my Sophomore year when I got a terrible case of asthma. I switched to managing the teams and helped when I could. I got to school before dawn most mornings (no joke) and stayed for two practices. I got ready for school, went and did homework during study hall, and then had after-school practice until late with the varsity team. To say that I had no life was an understatement. I did not get home until after 8 pm, then had dinner and crawled into bed, starting all over in the morning. However, I loved the girls, and they were my family. We did everything together, and that is how it should be. I never mentioned my private life to the girls. I did not want to worry them. My coaches had my back, and that is what matters. The sports never ended either because there was Track in the off-season. My head coach would take me to track meets after school with her to record in the booths. To say that I was a workaholic was an understatement. I was a perfectionistic, overthinking workaholic who was indecisive, lacked boundaries, and pleased people way too much. I lacked an identity, so I took off my senior year to focus on school. The girls did well that year, and I kicked myself for not being there for them. It is ironic how all the girls' varsity teams wanted me to help senior year, not just basketball but volleyball, soccer, and track. I will be the first to tell you that God cannot sit on the bench of your life; you must surrender control so He can lead.

My senior year was spent in the National Honor Society, especially volunteering. I spent most of my time in the career center, taking tests and learning about different jobs. I had always wanted to serve my country. I focused on studying for the ASVAB to attend the Air Force Academy.

My Testimony

When I found out I could not get in due to Post Traumatic Stress Disorder, I thought I would go the ROTC route in college. Due to unavoidable circumstances, I could not start ROTC until my junior year of college. When I got schizoaffective disorder during my first year of college, I could not join. I was told I had to be off medications for two years before joining. There went the military career I had always wanted.

Toward the end of high school, a neighborhood boy sexually assaulted me. I felt like trash and not good enough for God until I realized God was with me, grieving. I was a survivor, but it was not my fault. I did not even tell my mom about my sexual assault until years later when I was in college.

I went to college at Angelo State University and switched majors a few times. I had a group of friends, but I still felt empty and constantly lonely. My loved one would call me drunk all the time and tell me I was not going to make it in life and that I was a failure. I had a guy friend who felt sorry for me, so he introduced me to drinking and parties, and I got drunk one night and was raped after being drugged at a dance club. It turned into sexual abuse that lasted for about a year. Later that year, I joined the Assault Victim Services after the first rape situation as a volunteer. I did that for a while. I was still looking hard for a purpose and wore a mask. Everyone thought I was fine, but I was severely depressed and felt empty. I was so distressed about the abuse that I told no one I volunteered with. I stopped going to classes and slept all day while partying at night. I lost track of my life as I was either too drugged with alcohol or trying to help other victims out of a situation similar to mine, but I was not brave enough to get out of myself.

One night, I had a breakdown. I cut my arms up badly. I had inscribed "worthless" and "unloved" into my arms. Then, all of a sudden, I felt like I had bugs crawling in my arms. I tried to cut them out. I felt like I was in a whirlwind. I suddenly thought I was a warrior for God. I vowed to serve him and cut a cross into my arm. I almost took a bottle of pills, which could have killed me. After a while, I came to my senses. I realized the mess I had made and sought help from my dorm resident assistant. I had no idea she was a psychology major. She sat me down and talked with me, and I got help. I saw the school psychiatrist and got meds, making me feel like a zombie. My mom came to get me, and I moved home. I saw my psychiatrist and a counselor back in San Antonio.

In 2005, when I was 19 years old, I was admitted to my first mental health facility. I was diagnosed with schizoaffective disorder bipolar type, which has symptoms of schizophrenia and bipolar. I felt like hurting myself or others, and that scared me. I had delusions in which I believed I was the Bride of Christ, sensory hallucinations like voices, and mood swings. I also was very paranoid because I thought the government was after me. I was in and out of hospitals for years. I often wondered if I would ever make anything of myself. I felt so worthless and ashamed.

I had an illness that I knew nothing about that started consuming my life. I was left with no purpose or way out. That is when I decided that I had to do something about it and started attending the National Alliance on Mental Illness' peer-to-peer class. After a few years, my Christian counselor from home told me about a local 12-step group for hurts, habits, and hang-ups. I did both and learned how to cope with stress one day at a time.

In 2007, I heard about a ministry home for girls who had been abused or homeless. I went there for months. A group of girls my age would worship Jesus every morning and listen to a sermon. In the afternoons, we would read a book the counselor assigned and write a report. We ate fish or chicken daily, which got old because I could not eat fish. The organization promised I would get to see a professional counselor, but I did not. Someone with a divinity degree does not count as a Licensed Professional Counselor. It was also nearly impossible to see doctors and get meds filled regularly. With some of us having mental illness, there were problems. They also took our money when they said the program was free. Toward the end of my stay, two counselors came and spoke to me. They said I was not trying hard enough to change (less than six months to change with a lifelong mental illness) and let my shame and abuse control me. Soon after, they called me back into the office and closed the door. They started speaking in tongues and tried to pray the "demons" out of me because Satan caused schizoaffective, they thought. They forced me to speak in tongues as they placed their hands on me and prayed. I was terrified and made up words and wanted to cry. After, they sent me back to the group and told me not to tell anyone. Then, I was sent home a few days later. I was confused and wondered why God was mad at me. I had tried so hard. I kept asking, "Why God?"

I spent years in and out of hospitals without much help. Finally, I did get better. As I got back on track, I started to go to the University of Texas at San Antonio. This time, I met a great group of Christians who helped me learn who God truly was and that He loves me unconditionally. I realized Jesus never left me through the good and bad. I still had questions, but I believed. They told me that God had a purpose for me and truly cared for me. I could tell this was real because feelings do not determine faith, although I did have hope once again.

In 2012, I did have another hospital stay. I felt suicidal, so I went to an inpatient mental healthcare site. I received the best care possible. I went to classes where I learned about how to regulate my emotions, how to test hallucinations, and what dialectical behavior therapy was about. I received cognitive behavior therapy weekly and had a psychiatrist who helped me to realize what I wanted to do.

I completed my first degree from college in 2017. It took me 14 years on and off, but I did it. I could only afford a few classes at a time, and with my mental illness, it was much more challenging. I could take tests at a particular location and receive tutoring when needed. Graduating college was a significant milestone since some people could not believe it would happen, and I sometimes questioned it.

In July 2017, my family and I moved to North Texas, so my mom and stepdad could see the stepsiblings' kids and for me to get a new start. God allowed me enough experience with mental health to have great compassion for those who battle it, so I volunteered with my church's mental health ministry. We met multiple times monthly and discussed our illnesses and how we cope with them. In 2 Corinthians 1, the Bible talks about how God comforts me in my afflictions so that I can comfort those in any affliction. I used to volunteer at the local food pantry when I could. In James 1:27, the Bible talks about pure and undefiled religion as visiting orphans and widows in their distress. I love my life now and live to serve the one true God. I also have a positive outlook on life, but that does not mean I never struggle again.

My stepbrother, Colby, who is my hero, passed away from colon cancer in December 2018; A wife and two children survived him. God reassured me that he was in Heaven. At the funeral, I was comforted by all the stories shared about him and his testimony in helping other people. The Gospel was even shared. My stepsister, whom I admire, survived thyroid cancer a few years later. She is one of my inspirations.

On July 2nd, 2021, my stepdad was paralyzed in a home accident. Mom and I have been taking care of him ever since then. He gets stronger daily and can now walk on his own. I no longer resent him for his sarcasm, constant criticism, and negative attitude toward me. I have the daily opportunity to show God's kindness, strength, and mercy to those around me. I may be perplexed as Paul talks about in 2 Corinthians 4:7-10, but I am also a fragile but functional piece of pottery representing Jesus to the world. We are currently getting along well.

I started attending a 12-step program for hurts, habits, and hang-ups in 2021 in North Texas. In this group, I learned that my secrets did not make me damaged goods as I thought. It was like in the Bible when Joseph said, "What you meant for harm, God meant for good (Genesis 50:20)." Jesus rescued and redeemed me. I have beauty for ashes. I am a precious daughter, a royal priest, more than a conqueror, and an ambassador for Christ.

I came into this group, battling three decades of verbal, emotional, physical, sexual, and mental abuse from someone I love, who I believe is an alcoholic. I thought I would be a good child if I honored them by listening. I learned through this program how to get rid of my victim mentality, stop blaming others, and, most importantly, I forgave this loved one on June 20, 2021. This was radical. I felt like a weight had been lifted off my shoulders. I do not want revenge anymore; I see them through God's eyes with love. God's steadfast love and mercy are greater than any sin, and he promises forgiveness in Lamentations 3.

Working on both harm by me and toward me was very hard. I had feared men more than God, but not anymore. In 2021, I went on a retreat with my church. There, I wrote God a note about how sorry I was for projecting my loved one's character onto Him. I saw God as punishing and angry. Now, I have experienced His love and grace and see Him in a new way. I also threw that letter and a notecard about my amends into the fire. I am completely free and starting to love others as God sees them.

I can have conversational prayer throughout the day with God, listen to and sing worship music, praise God while spending time in nature, gather with Christians to glorify God and encourage one another, and volunteer. I have experienced healthy, authentic relationships with other Christians during this group. Thankfully, God gave me his people, the Church, and the Holy Spirit to love, support, and guide me in my relationships with others (Ephesians 4:11-16).

I still live with my parents since I am disabled. I take my meds daily and have a routine. I still do counseling, which helps me every day. I take life day to day but still have challenges that life throws my way. I believe in God and that He sent His one and only son, Jesus Christ, to die on the cross for my sins, and I am learning to trust Him daily. He is my rock and salvation. He was there with me every step of the way, even when I doubted and failed Him. God does not leave you in your pain; He redeems it. Jesus saved me.

I continue to fight today for my God-given worth, sometimes with setbacks, but I am in recovery now due to my faith in Jesus Christ. I lament my fears and problems to God, and my illness becomes manageable with my coping skills, medication, and counseling. I pray to God for the strength to carry on and find words of encouragement in His Word. I also love worshipping and fellowshipping with other Christians at my church. My time, talents, energy, and gifts will be used to honor, glorify, serve, and love God.

APPENDIX C

Letter to Self Written While Hospitalized in 2012

Amy,

So, you think you are sad, but I see a friendly and generous person. Moreover, how can you be lonely when you are never alone because God is always watching over you? You are a good student and responsible, but seriously, lighten up. Why be worried? You are courageous and an ambitious, hard worker. Fearful in the least because I see a strong, loyal peacemaker. You are beautiful inside and out. I see an intelligent and creative person, not someone who is dumb. Do not let your illness define you. Are you having anger issues? Put it to good use and go volunteer. You think you are shy and quiet but are outgoing when you want to be. Lacking energy, be adventurous. Moreover, who says you are hard on people because compassion is in your nature? You are not a failure because of how far you have gotten. I know you want to be happy, honest, optimistic, able to express feelings, content, and patient. Whoa! Hold on, tiger! One thing at a time, but good goals. Believe in yourself because you are loved and awesome. You are an amazing, wonderful person. Plus, you will make it. Be willing to take a stand. Moreover, do not get too comfortable because you will make a difference. Keep holding on and look within yourself to see who you are.

Love,
Tough Cookie (myself)

> *Psalms 40:1-3 "I waited patiently for the Lord to help me, and he turned to me and heard my cry. He lifted me out of the pit of despair, out of the mud and the mire. He set my feet on solid ground and steadied me as I walked along. He has given me a new song to sing, a hymn of praise to our God. Many will see what he has done and be amazed. They will put their trust in the Lord."*

APPENDIX D

Prophecy by Jane Hamon, an Author and Prophetess, on Feb 27, 2008

I received this word for word prophecy while at a home for abused girls and girls with mental health concerns. This explains what God has been trying to edify and build me up with for years. I have tried never to forget this, especially since all that happened is not God's fault. This has really impacted my life.

The Lord says "Daughter, I have given you a very sharp mind, one that likes to reason, analyze, know the truth, and even questions. You say why this and why that? Even with others around you, you ask why. Inquiring minds want to know. I put that questioning inside of you because you are a lover of truth. But in the midst of the questioning, the enemy came in and brought skepticism and tried to undermine your faith when I have actually given you an incredible gift of faith. I have put inside of you the ability to have strong faith and the ability to have strong reasoning abilities. This is going to be a powerful one-two punch in my Kingdom because you are not just going to be able to present the spiritual principles but the reasoning behind it. That will give people the ability to overcome humanism and their own human reasoning and be able to actually be reconciled with me. Because I have given that to you, all hell rose up against you to try and shut that down. You went through your own crisis of faith and you wondered if I was real and if

I was there. It seemed like every circumstance around you started speaking other than that to you. The enemy started saying that "If the Lord is real, why did this happen? And why did he let that happen?" and the Lord says, "Daughter, I don't let things happen. The Word says that there is an enemy in this world that knew he was out to destroy you. There was even one time where the enemy just wanted to snuff your life right out and I extended my hand out and said no way and delivered you from death into light. There have actually been times throughout your life when that has been the case, where death came knocking at your door when destruction came and the enemy thought at one point that if he couldn't kill you physically, he would just kill your soul by shutting your soul and mind down. He threw everything he could against you to try and cause that to happen by trying to shut you down from life and to lose faith not only in me but in yourself for a while. You started because you lost faith in me and others. But I actually put a strong gift of faith inside of you and I am resurrecting that gift of faith that goes along with reasoning. There are a lot of question marks that you have had. But I am going to turn your question marks into exclamation points. I am gonna give you the ability to communicate through all this. The enemy tried to shut your communication down but I am giving you an anointing to communicate. You are gonna be very gifted in writing, speaking, sharing, and reasoning. You kind of got yourself trapped for a while and you reasoned yourself into a corner but we are breaking you out of the corner and releasing that faith inside of you that is going to be able to look at things that are impossible as possible because that is what faith is. I have given you the ability to look at some impossible situations as possible that right now are kind of in front of your face and you are saying how God. The question turned from why to how. I know how daughter. Trust me. I am walking you on a narrow path but don't get frustrated, discouraged, or antsy. Please let me walk you on this narrow path. Finish the course. Because right now you

Prophecy by Jane Hamon, an Author and Prophetess, on Feb 27, 2008

are almost at a point where you are saying "I don't know if I can go further." But I want you to know that I am gonna take you by the hand and pull you further past your reasoning and excuses because I created something inside of you that so hungers for truth that you are not going to be satisfied until you know the fullness of who I am and who I am in you. And so the Spirit of the Lord says "Daughter, know that I am doing a good work and gonna take you all the way through to completion. I am not gonna let you quit. Actually, you are not really a quitter. But there is something inside of you that is clicking and going through the motions. I am gonna put that full passion inside of you, one that will see my purposes fulfilled." Now, Father, I thank you Lord that there is a release that is gonna come through her and those things that have dogged her path will move. I thank you Father that you are releasing her from that death spirit and all the things that happened externally that the enemy sent against her from people and circumstances that tried to take her internally and tried to get her to take her life. I thank you, Lord, that you are delivering her out of that place of death, which has no place in her or dominion over her, into that place of life because victory is her's. I activate that gift of faith, Father God. And thank you Lord for that supernatural faith that moves mountains, Lord, in this season of time. I bless her for finishing the course, and race, and going all the way to completion. In Jesus' Name, Amen.

APPENDIX E
Prayers to God while in the 12 Step Program

Dear Abba,

As I sit here praying, I am afraid of falling apart again. I know that I am always asking why this and how that, but you just want me to trust you. You say that with man, it is impossible, but with You it is possible. I know I struggle with not knowing who I am without my disorder. Maybe I was too comfortable with my mental illnesses, which I have had since middle school. I often feel misunderstood from my feelings to my behavior. I know that I deserve to do more than just survive. I still struggle with the fear of what-ifs, which can paralyze me.

1. What if my parents die? Will I be homeless with a mental illness?

2. What if I lose my battle to suicide? Will I still be in Heaven with You?

3. What if I fail to complete the race set before me?

4. What if my support system fails?

5. What if my medications stop working?

6. What if my love for You goes cold? Will you still love me like Hosea?

7. What if all I know is being abused? Will I learn my lesson?

8. Will I ever find true love?

9. What happens if I stand up for myself? Will I be a good advocate?

10. When all else falls apart, will I still stand?

You tell me I am Yours always; that You love me and will take care of me for all eternity. Please give me the faith to believe You! I want to be so in love with You that this world just fades away. You say seek me with all of my heart. Your servant and daughter are right here! Please explain to me unspeakable things. Help me to remember the Hall of Faith in Hebrews. There was Abraham counting the stars, Joshua marching around Jericho, Noah waiting on the rain to stop, Moses standing up for Your people, and David a man after Your heart. Then You, Jesus, are my life, my love, my everything who died for me. Oh and who could forget John who was beloved like me and Peter who walked on water, and Stephen the first martyr? My favorite after You, Jesus, was Job who never cursed You even though he lost everything or Ruth, the outcast, who was accepted. I will never be perfect, loved by everyone, or liked every time, but I will show up, be true to myself, and do my best. I choose today and all the days after to just be joyful because I am stronger than I think. Strength comes from overcoming something I never thought that I could. It is time to let go of the labels that often define me. There is freedom in knowing that I'll never be perfect, but I can be joyful living my best life. I will always be more than enough through You, Jesus Christ.

Love,
Your Daughter Amy

Father,

Oh, Lord! I have questioned your love for me and doubted your good nature. You give grace in moments of honesty and brokenness. I have failed you and tried to control everything. I struggle with self-hate from being abused and abandoned. I seek others instead of you. Please forgive me for my idolatry. I am crying out to you for my heart aches. I have betrayed you. I long for your forgiveness, mercy, and grace. I am here because you have been pursuing me all along. You are concerned for my heart. I long for joy, satisfaction, and peace. The truths in your word encourage and comfort me, but I am lost. Please rescue me, heal me, and restore me to my purpose. I have strayed. I need your word, the Holy Spirit, and your people to fully recover. I feel alone and overwhelmed by my pain and struggles. I have to take it one day at a time. I humbly ask you, God, for your Spirit to change my heart and mind to follow you fully. I want to pursue righteousness, faith, love, and peace. Please help me apply your word to my life and develop relationships with others worthy of you. You love me not because of my goodness or because I have earned your love but because you are good. You love me just as I am. I seek you! Thank you, Jesus Christ, for being my Lord and Savior and making me right with you, God. I long to know you better. I want to cherish my adoption by you, Lord. I cannot wait for the day we can walk and talk face-to-face. May I honor and glorify you going forward. I surrender all to you! Thank you for knowing and loving me!

Love,
Your Daughter Amy

Father,

You say to ask for wisdom, and I shall receive it. What is the root cause of my regret of the past and fear of the future? I am paralyzed! My shame and loneliness haunt me. I long for clear direction from you. I will wait patiently for your guidance and strength. Maybe my next step is simple: praying, going for a nature walk, or encouraging someone. It could be as easy as taking one step at a time. I know you love me and want what is best for me. I need you to protect, carry, and direct me through the storms of life. I still struggle with my abuse, abandonment, and self-hate. I miss all the people I have lost. As you bring me through this, may I be honest? I chose to trust and rely on you, God. Thank you for everything! Amen.

Love,
Your Daughter Amy

Father,

As I take steps toward change, I know I will face hardships. I pray that you give me the strength and courage to change my surroundings and relationships that harm my life. Most of my relationships are beneficial. Please help me to determine healthy boundaries, as some people have crossed the line many times. I also seek your guidance on developing friendships that will encourage and strengthen me. I know isolating myself during times of weakness is easy, and I am afraid I will get hurt if vulnerable. I do not have it all together. I should not hide my weaknesses and failures. I wonder what life would be like if I loved you wholeheartedly and valued the long-term best interests of others above my own. Help me to love you and others. I know that sometimes I compare myself to others or blame others when I get bitter and angry. However, I know you can bring order from chaos and save what has been lost. I am glad you can graciously provide me with everything I need. For so long, I have feared the future and being homeless with a mental illness. Everything will be good with you at the lead. Please help me to learn more about you as I read your word. I want to hear and do your word. Please help me to understand your directions for my life and apply them. Thank you for everything!

Love,
Your Daughter Amy

Father,

As I trust you, I hope you faithfully restore me to whom you designed me to be. Please help me to see you at work, which will strengthen me. Faith will lead to hope, allowing me to view my future better. My broken faith, with damaged trust and shattered hope, will be no more. Thank you for loving me and helping me. Please help me not to worry, which is one of my most destructive habits. Help me to pray and appeal with thanksgiving to you. May I cast all my anxieties on you for you care for me? I am choosing to trust you for the future and live in the present because I know that you are in control even when it does not feel like it or circumstances do not make sense to me. You love me, have a plan for me, and know how I can have peace through difficulties. Please take away any interfering distractions, fears, or attitudes and draw me close to you. I want to draw closer to and know you better during my dependence on you. Please help me to practice daily gratitude and be aware of my blessings, for every good and perfect gift is from you. I know that I need the involvement, encouragement, and counsel of others as I walk through the storms. I cannot wait to be loved in my brokenness. Please, Lord, give me strength and courage. Also, please increase my faith and give me hope for a better future with you.

Love,
Your Daughter Amy

Father,

I ask for guidance on responding to those who have hurt me. Free me from any resentment I have held against you and others. Sometimes I bury the pain and then lash out at others or self-harm. Holding on to pain or misusing it enslaves me to anger, mistrust, and despair. Forgiveness does not mean you forget the hurt or ignore justice by allowing someone to get away with harmful actions. It simply means that I release them from the debt caused by their destructive actions. I trust you, God, for justice instead of trying to get even. You, Lord, have been patient to delay justice for my sins and now forgive my sins through Christ. Thank you! Contentment, peace, and life are genuinely possible through you! Amen!

Love,
Your Daughter Amy

Father,

Please help me to trust that you will be close to my broken heart and that, in time, you will heal my wounds. Please help me to do whatever it takes to be well. I know Your will through the Bible. By reading, hearing, and learning about Your heart and mind, you change my heart and mind. When I grasp your love for me and realize that you want what is best for me, you transform my desire to follow your will. Please help me to know and follow your good, acceptable, and perfect will. God, you want to help hurting people. Please give me the heart of a servant. Help me to follow Christ by considering others' needs, great and small. Strengthen me to care for them as you do. Help me experience life's fullness in you, Christ, when I follow you and walk in your ways. God, you bring hope, encouragement, strength, and comfort when I allow myself to be known and become willing to know others. Please help me to trust you since you are in control.

Love,
Your Daughter Amy

Abba (Father),

I approach in faith and humility. I want fellowship and intimacy with you. I desire to love and be loved. You are my counselor, full of mercy, grace, and unconditional love. You provide for my every need. I seek your will. May I obey you and be one with you. May I share your love for others as I was created to love. Thank you for healing me!

With Love and Admiration,
Your Daughter Amy

Abba (Father),

Your love makes possible the impossible. When we face seemingly impossible situations, remind us of Your love and its possibilities. Because knowing how absolute is my dependence on You, I find peace of mind. I have tasted Your love. I have known Your compassion. I have experienced Your patience, and I am filled with gratefulness. May today I bring glory and honor to You. Amen.

Love,
Your Daughter Amy

Acknowledgements

To My North and South Texas Friends,

Thanks to my friends! Lately, the Lord has been revealing to me how blessed I am to have such wonderful friends in my life. I have gone through some crazy times in recent years from emotional to physical trials, and yet through it all I have been blessed to have the most amazing love and support. Thanks for helping me through a rough time in my life. If y'all had not prayed over me countless times, I don't know if I would have made it. For all of my friends who love me beyond what I could ever deserve, thank you! And for your countless smiles, phone calls, and e-mails that brighten my life everyday, thank you! I do not know what I would do without each one of you close to my heart and in my prayers. I am proud to know each one of you. Thanks again!

John 15:13 "Greater love has no one than this, that he lay down his life for his friends."

"There is a miracle of friendship that dwells within the heart. And you don't know how it happens or where it gets its start. But the happiness it brings you always gives a special lift. Then you realize that friendship is God's most perfect gift." – Anonymous

"In poverty and other misfortunes of life, true friends are a sure refuge. The young they keep out of mischief; to the old they are a comfort and aid in their weakness, and those in the prime of life they incite to noble deeds." – Aristotle

"Be courteous to all, but intimate with few, and let those few be well tried before you give them your confidence. True friendship is a plant of slow growth, and must undergo and withstand the shocks of adversity before it is entitled to the appellation." – George Washington

"Do not walk behind me; I may not lead. Do not walk in front of me; I may not follow. Just walk beside me and be my friend." – Albert Camus

"A real friend is one who walks in when the rest of the world walks out." – Anonymous

"A friend is one who knows you and loves you just the same." – Elbert Hubbard

Speaking to Social Workers for a Second...

Thank y'all for what you do! We could not do this without you as a key piece of the treatment team. My social worker is right about positive aspects of being a social worker including giving back, helping others, forming a one-on-one relationship with clients, making progress with clients, having self-agency, collaborating with coworkers, and talking with the boss. Negative aspects can include hearing and seeing hardships, not being able to do more, and having to separate yourself during crises with healthy boundaries. She is right about social workers needing to have themselves together mentally and emotionally, and being nonjudgmental and open-minded while knowing your own personal biases.

My social worker is absolutely right when she said, "A small act of kindness, a few encouraging words, and just letting someone know help is out there can make a big difference. It can be the lifeline that pulls them back from the edge." While showing the client the way out, believing in and being proud of them can pull them back from the edge. This is how my social workers brought me back many times. God turns our small sacrifices into something beautiful for a world desperate for peace and compassion.

I do believe that social workers should network and connect with other social workers regarding resources. They could come up with a list of resources in the local community (description of local non-profits and community-based organizations with phone numbers and addresses) and put them on a flyer to hand out to clients or other social workers.

I know being on Medicaid with a mental illness and living in poverty has prevented me from navigating the waters for help, but my social worker encourages me to never give up when it is hard. Policies do impact clients, like me, on a regular basis. Activism is key here and taking what you have learned working in the community to the individuals and families is extremely important. I know volunteering has helped me a lot in confidence building and brings me much gratitude, which in turn keeps me motivated.

There are numerous ways to involve macro practice, like advocating for clients and participating in activism, into micro practice with individuals and families. I want to work as a Licensed Clinical Social Worker at a nonprofit in Fort Worth. Since I want to do direct practice in the mental health field, I could suggest to an individual or family to join the local or state National Alliance on Mental Illness. Clients can take a peer-to-peer course for people with mental illness, and families can take the family-to-family course for families of people with mental illness. I think learning about your mental illness and talking to others about it could help motivate someone with it to get better and know what to do in hard times. I believe community education courses like that would build confidence and self-advocacy skills. Once a year, the National Alliance on Mental Illness goes to the state capital to share their testimonies and stories with House and Senate members. This helps improve policy for people with mental illness, and I could recommend doing this with them. The National Alliance on Mental Illness also has veteran classes and school presentations that involve people with mental illness. Empowerment and advocacy can get a client unstuck. It does build confidence and effective problem-solving skills. I know my personal LCSW guides me to make better decisions for myself and helps me take the lead in my life, especially after being abused for most of my life. You could start the client on finding out what their likes and dislikes are and go from there.

References

Bailey, Aubrey. "Coping Mechanisms: Everything You Need to Know." Very Well Health. January 1, 2024. https://www.verywellhealth.com/coping-mechanisms-5272135.

"Behavior." APA Dictionary of Psychology. American Psychological Association, Accessed January 1, 2024. https://dictionary.apa.org/behavior.

"Boundary." APA Dictionary of Psychology. American Psychological Association, Accessed January 1, 2024. https://dictionary.apa.org/boundary.

"Cognitive Behavior Theory." APA Dictionary of Psychology. American Psychological Association, Accessed January 1, 2024. https://dictionary.apa.org/cognitive-behavior-theory.

Comiskey, Joel. "What Was the New Testament Church Like?" Christianity Today. Retrieved January 1, 2023, from https://www.smallgroups.com/articles/2015/what-was-new-testament-church-like.html

"Compassion." Dictionary.Com. Accessed January 1, 2024. https://www.dictionary.com/browse/compassion.

"Coping Mechanism." APA Dictionary of Psychology. American Psychological Association, Accessed January 1, 2024. https://dictionary.apa.org/coping-mechanism.

References

"Dialectical Behavior Therapy." APA Dictionary of Psychology. American Psychological Association, Accessed January 1, 2024. https://dictionary.apa.org/dialectical-behavior-therapy.

Duckworth, Ken. You Are Not Alone: The NAMI Guide to Navigating Mental Health. First Edition. New York: Zando, 2022.

Ferentz, Lisa. "USING CARESS TO WORK WITH SELF-DESTRUCTIVE BEHAVIORS." The Ferentz Institute. Accessed January 1, 2024. https://www.theferentzinstitute.com/2021/03/15/using-caress-work-self-destructive-behaviors/.

Holy Bible, New Living Translation, copyright 1996, 2004, 2015 by Tyndale House Foundation. All rights reserved.

Hunt, June. Verbal & Emotional Abuse: Victory Over Verbal and Emotional Abuse. Fifteenth Edition. California: Rose Publishing, 2016.

Jones, Heather. Dialectical Behavior Therapy vs. Cognitive Behavioral Therapy. Very Well Health. October 15, 2022. https://www.verywellhealth.com/dialectical-behavior-therapy-vs-cognitive-behavioral-therapy-uses-benefits-side-effects-and-more-5323767

National Institute of Mental Health. (2023). Understanding Psychosis (NIH Publication No. 23-MH-8110). U.S. Department of Health and Human Services, National Institutes of Health. Retrieved April 23, 2023, from https://www.nimh.nih.gov/health/topics/schizophrenia/raise/fact-sheet-early-warning-signs-of-psychosis

N., Sam M.S., "BEHAVIOR," in PsychologyDictionary.org, April 7, 2013, https://psychologydictionary.org/behavior/ (accessed February 24, 2024)

Stein, Samantha. The Importance of Community. Psychology Today. July 18, 2023. https://www.psychologytoday.com/us/blog/what-the-wild-things-are/202307/the-importance-of-community

Van Horn, Hannah. Journaling About Feelings: How to Explore and Express Emotions. April 26, 2023. https://dayoneapp.com/blog/journaling-about-feelings/

Welch, Edward T. Shame Interrupted: How God Lifts the Pain of Worthlessness & Rejection. First Edition. North Carolina: New Growth Press, 2012.

World Bank. "World Bank Group–International Development, Poverty, & Sustainability," 2023. https://www.worldbank.org/en/home.

Printed in the USA
CPSIA information can be obtained
at www.ICGtesting.com
CBHW050615081124
17080CB00039B/265